THE DEVELOPMENT OF WESTERN MUSIC

AN ANTHOLOGY

VOLUME I

From Ancient Times
through the Baroque Era

Third Edition

THE DEVELOPMENT OF WESTERN MUSIC

AN ANTHOLOGY

Edited by

K MARIE STOLBA

Professor of Music, Emerita
Indiana University—Purdue
University Fort Wayne

VOLUME I

**From Ancient Times
through the Baroque Era**

Boston   Burr Ridge, IL   Dubuque, IA   Madison, WI   New York   San Francisco   St. Louis
Bangkok   Bogotá   Caracas   Lisbon   London   Madrid
Mexico City   Milan   New Delhi   Seoul   Singapore   Sydney   Taipei   Toronto

McGraw-Hill

A Division of the McGraw-Hill Companies

THE DEVELOPMENT OF WESTERN MUSIC, An Anthology, Volume I, Third Edition

✪ This book is printed on recycled, acid-free paper containing 10% postconsumer waste.

1 2 3 4 5 6 7 8 9 0 QPD/QPD 9 0 9 8

ISBN 0-697-32868-6

Publisher: *Phil Butcher*
Sponsoring editor: *Christopher Freitag*
Developmental editor: *JoElaine Retzler*
Marketing manager: *David Patterson*
Project manager: *Marilyn Rothenberger*
Production supervisor: *Mary Haas*
Designer: *Mary Christianson*
Art editor: *Joyce Watters*
Compositor: *A-R Editions, Inc.*
Typeface: *10/12 Berkeley*
Printer: *Quebecor, Inc.*

Cover designer: Maureen McCutcheon

Library of Congress Cataloging Card Number 97-75923

www.mhhe.com

S. D. G.

Contents

TRANSITION TO RENAISSANCE

RENAISSANCE

Preface to the Third Edition

This third edition of *The Development of Western Music: An Anthology* is a two-volume historical anthology of music specifically designed to present music to be studied in conjunction with the third edition of the text *The Development of Western Music: A History*. With few exceptions, the selections are complete movements or complete compositions. The works are presented in the Anthology in the same order in which they are mentioned or discussed in the History text. Volume I contains selections representative of music from Ancient Times through the Baroque Era; Volume II holds compositions characteristic of the Preclassic and Classic Eras, the transition from Classic to Romantic music, and Romantic and Modern works. Sets of sound recordings of the selections in the Anthology have been prepared and are available in either CD or cassette form for use with the Anthology and the History text. The music is printed in the Anthology in its original key; however, the recording, particularly of vocal music, may be in a different key. The recordings are intended to be a historical presentation; when feasible, recordings using period instruments have been selected. Because tuning was not standardized prior to 1700, there may be some instances in which the recorded music sounds "out of tune" to modern ears.

Texts of vocal music are presented in their original language, with English translation. Most of the translations of poetic and prose texts are my own; the work of other persons is acknowledged. I am indebted to Father Dick John of St. Francis College, Fort Wayne, for assistance with some medieval Latin texts containing particular ecclesiastical expressions, and to Miguel Roig-Francolí for help in translating some Spanish and Galician poetry.

Although this Anthology was designed to complement the History text, the Anthology is complete in itself, and its selections can serve as works for study and analysis in Form and Analysis, Music Literature, Music Theory, or other music courses.

It is impossible to name all those who contributed to this project. From time to time, several of my colleagues, particularly, the late John Loessi, and Masson Robertson, have loaned me music from their personal libraries. Many libraries have shared their holdings with me. Great demands have been made upon the Music Library at Indiana University, Bloomington, and thanks are due especially to Music Librarians R. Michael Fling and David Lasocky and the reference assistants, who responded promptly to my requests for materials. The librarians in the Inter-Library Loan/Document Delivery Services department at Helmke Library, IPFW, were most helpful in procuring materials. Marilyn Grush, Larry Griffin, and Christine Smith spent much time helping me research sources there. I wish to express my gratitude to Kenneth Balthaser, who made available the facilities at the IPFW Learning Resource Center and the services of its technicians in the preparation of camera-ready proof, particularly, Roberta Sandy Shadle.

Where no specific modern publication is cited, the music was transcribed and/or edited from original sources. McGraw-Hill and I are grateful to the persons and publishers who have granted permission to reprint, edit, or adapt material for which they hold copyright. I wish to express my appreciation also to my editors at McGraw-Hill, who carefully considered my requests, and to my book team and all other persons who were involved in the production of these volumes.

K Marie Stolba
Fort Wayne, Indiana

1 A HURRIAN CULT SONG FROM ANCIENT UGARIT

Anonymous (c. 1400 B.C.)

Transcription and arrangement
by Anne Draffkorn Kilmer

[x]* ha-nu-ta ni-ya-ša zi-we ši-nu-te zu-tu-ri-ya u-bu-ga-ra

ku-dur-ni ta-šal kil-la zi-li šip-ri hu-ma-ru-hat u-wa-ri

wan-da-ni-ta u-ku-ri kur-kur-ta (i)-šal-la u-la-li kab-gi al-lib-gi ši-rit mur-nu-šu

we-šal ta-tib ti-ši-ya u-nu-ga kab-ši-li u-nu-gat ak-li

šam-šam me-lil uk-lal tu-nu-ni-ta-ka ha-nu-ka ka-li-ta-nil ni-ka-la

nih(u)-ra-šal ha-na ha-nu-te-ti att-(a)yaš-tal at-ta-ri tae-ti ha-nu-ka

[x x x x x x x] -ša-ti we-we ha-nu-ku

*x denotes broken or effaced portion of tablet

Because knowledge of the Hurrian language is still imperfect, no translation of these hymn lyrics is available. The word *nikala* indicates that the song is a hymn to the wife of the moon god, her name being Nikal (Nikkal). The words *wešal tatib tišya* translate "Thou lovest them in [thy] heart" and the closing words *Wewe hanuku* have been translated as "born of thee."

See DWM p. 7, and Fig. 1.3.

2 FIRST DELPHIC HYMN TO APOLLO

Anonymous (c. 130 B.C.)

A

Κέ — κλυθ,' Ἑ — λι — κῶ — να βα — θύ — δεν — δρον αἳ λα — χε — τε, Δι — ὸς
Ke — klyth, Heli — kō — na ba — thy — den — dron hai la — che — te, Di — os

ἔ — ρι βρό — μουου θύ — γα — τρες εὐ — ω — λέ — νοι. Μό — λε — τε, συν — ό —
e — ri bro — mou thy — ga — tres ey — ō — le — noi. Mo — le — te, syn — o —

ματ — μον ἵ — να Φοιοῖ — βον ᾠ — δαῖ — σι μέλ — Ψη — τε χρυ —
mai — mon hi — na Phoi — bon ō — dai — si mel — pse — te, chry —

— σε — ο — κό — μαν. Ὃς ἀ — νὰ δι — κό — ρυν — βα Παρ — νασ — σί — δος
— se — o — ko — man. Hos a — na di — ko — ryn — ba Par — nas — si — dos

τᾶσ — δε πε — τέ — ρας ἕ — δραν ἅμ' ἀ — γα — κλυ — ται — εῖς Δελ — φί — σι — ιν
tas — de pe — te — ras he — dran ham' a — ga — kly — tais Del — phi — sin

Κα — στα — λί — δος ἔ — ου — ύ — δρου νά — ματ' ἐ — πι — νί — σε — ται,
Ka — sta — li — dos ey — hy — drou na — mat' e — pi — nis — se — tai,

Δελ — φόν ἀ — νὰ πρωῶ — να μααν τε — τεῖ — ον ἐφ — έ — πων πά — γον.
Del — phon a — na prō — na man — tei — on eph — e — pōn pa — gon.

B

Πά — ρα κλυ — τὰ με — γα — λό — πο — λις Αθ — θὶς εὐ — χαι — εῖ — σι, φε — ρό —
Pa — ra kly — ta me — ga — lo — po — lis At — this eu — chai — si phe — ro —

πλοι — ο — ναί ου — σα Τρι — τω — νί — δος δἀ — πε — δον ἀ —
— ploi — o — nai — ou — sa Tri — to — ni — dos da — pe — don a —

θραυ — στον! ἀ — γί — οις δὲ βώ — μοι — σιν Ἅ — φαι στος αἰ — εῖ
thrau — ston! Ha — gi — ois de bo — moi — sin Ha — phai — stos ai —

θει — νέ — ων μῆ — ρα ταυ — ού — ρων ὁ — μουου δὲ νιν Ἄ — ραψ
thei — ne — on me — ra tau — ou — ron ho — mou de nin A — raps

See DWM p. 8, and Fig. 1.4.

α - τμὸς ἐς Ὄ - λυμ - πον ἀ - να - κιδ - να - ται. Λι - γὺ δὲ λω -
a - tmos es O - lym - pon a - na - kid - na - tai. Li - gv de lo -

- το - ὸς βρέ - μων αἰ - ει - ό - λοι - οις μέ - λε - σιν ῷ -
- tos bre - mon ai o - lois me - le - sin o -

- δα - ἀν κρέ - κει, χρυ - σέ - α δ' ἁ - δύ - θρους κί - θα - ρις ὕ -
- dan kre - kei chry - se - a d'ha - dy - throus ki - tha - ris hym -

- μνοι - σιν ἀ - να - μέλ - πε - ται.
- noi - sin a - na - mel - pe - tai.

Hearken, fair-armed daughters of Zeus the loud Thunderer, who have your appointed home on deep-wooded Helicon; come that you may honor with dance and song your brother, Phoebus of the golden tresses, who comes up to his abode on the twin peaks of this rock of Parnassus here, in the company of the far-famed women of Delphi, to visit the streams of Castalia with its fair waters, frequenting his prophetic hill upon the Delphic crag.

Behold! Attica's great and famous city, which by the prayers of the warrior maiden Tritonis dwells in a plain inviolate! On the holy altars the Firegod burns the thighs of young bulls, while the fragrance of Arabia is wafted to Olympus; and the flute in clear, shrill notes pipes its song with varied tunes; and the sweet-voiced lyre of gold strikes up the hymns.

But the whole swarm of musicians who have their home in Attica sing hymns of praise to you, famous player of the yre, son of mighty Zeus, beside this your snow-capped hill; for you reveal to all mortals holy oracles which cannot lie, since you took the prophetic tripod which the fierce serpent used to gard, at that itme when you pierced with your shafts its dapled, writhing form, until the monster, emitting harsh hisses thick and fast, breathed out its life likewise.

But when the War-god of the Celts . . .

—Edna M. Hooker

3 EPITAPH OF SEIKILOS

(c. second century B.C.)

a Greek Notation

As long as you live, be happy;
do not grieve at all.
Life's span is short;
time exacts the final reckoning.

b Modern Transcription

Ho-son dzĕs phai - nou,

mē - den ho-lōs sy ly - poū.

Pros o - li-gon es - ti to dzēn,

to te-los ho chro-nos ap-ai - tei.

See DWM p. 8, and Fig. 1.5.

SALVE, REGINA, Marian Antiphon

Anonymous

Modern Transcription

Gregorian Chant Notation

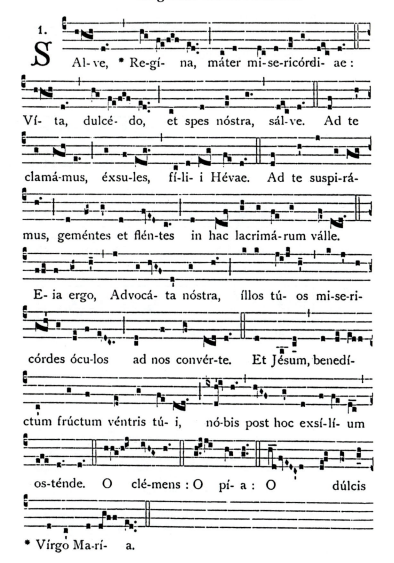

See DWM p. 30, 39.

Salve, Regina, mater misericordiae:
Vita, dulcedo, et spes nostra, salve.
Ad te clamamus, exsules, filii Hevae.
Ad te suspiramus, gementes et flentes in hac lacrimarum valle.
Eia ergo, Advocata nostra, illos tuos misericordes oculos ad nos converte.
Et Jesum, benedictum fructum ventris tui, nobis post hoc exsilium ostende.
O clemens: O pia: O dulcis Virgo Maria.

Hail, Queen, compassionate mother:
Our life, sweetness, and hope, hail!
To you we cry aloud, exiles, children of Eve.
To you we send [our] sighs, groaning and weeping in this vale of tears.
Then, our Advocate, turn your compassionate eyes toward us.
And, after this exile, show us Jesus, the blessed fruit of your womb.
O merciful: O holy: O sweet Virgin Mary.

probásti me, et cognoví-sti me : tu cognoví-sti sessi-ó-nem me- am, et re-surrecti-ó-nem me-am.

5 MISSA IN DOMINICA RESURRECTIONIS
(Mass for Easter Sunday)
Anonymous

Gló-ri-a Patri et Fí-li-o, et Spi-rí-tu-i Sancto. * Sic-ut e-rat in princí-pi-o, et nunc, et semper, et in sæ-cu-la sæ-cu-ló-rum. A-men.

Introit

Ps. 138, 18. 5. 6 et 1-2

E-SURRE-XI, * et adhuc te-cum sum, al-le-lú- ia: po-su-í-sti su- per me ma- num tu- am, al- le-lú- ia: mi-rá- bi-lis fa- cta est sci- én-ti-a tu- a, alle-lú- ia, al- le-lú- ia. *Ps.* Dó-mi-ne

Kyrie

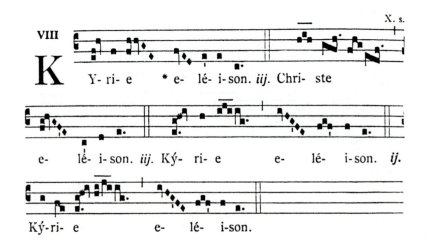

X. s.

VIII

KY-ri-e * e-lé-i-son. *iij.* Chri-ste e-lé-i-son. *iij.* Ký-ri-e e-lé-i-son. *ij.* Ký-ri-e e-lé-i-son.

See DWM pp. 30, 40, 45–48, and Plate 4.

Gloria

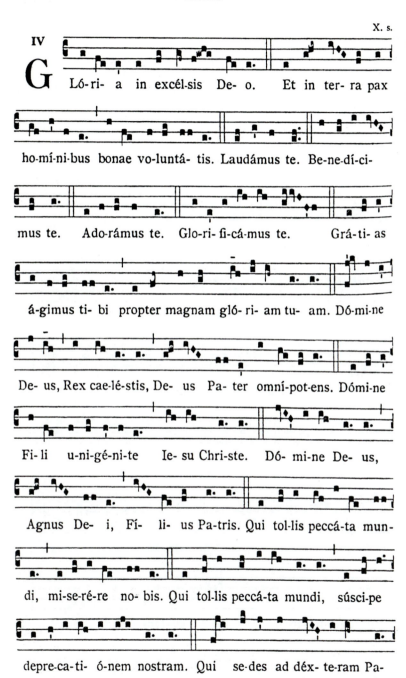

IV X. s.

G Ló-ri- a in excél-sis De- o. Et in ter- ra pax

ho-mí-ni-bus bonae vo-luntá- tis. Laudámus te. Be-ne-dí-ci-

mus te. Ado-rámus te. Glo-ri- fi-cá-mus te. Grá-ti- as

á-gimus ti- bi propter magnam gló- ri- am tu- am. Dó-mi-ne

De- us, Rex cae-lé-stis, De- us Pa- ter omní-pot-ens. Dómi-ne

Fi- li u-ni-gé-ni-te Ie-su Chri-ste. Dó- mi-ne De- us,

Agnus De- i, Fí- li- us Pa-tris. Qui tol-lis peccá-ta mun-

di, mi-se-ré-re no- bis. Qui tol-lis peccá-ta mundi, súsci-pe

depre-ca-ti- ó-nem nostram. Qui se-des ad déx- te-ram Pa-

tris, mi-se-ré- re no- bis. Quóni- am tu so-lus sanctus, Tu

so-lus Dó- mi-nus. Tu so-lus Altíssimus, Ie- su Chri-ste.

Cum Sancto Spí- ri- tu, in gló- ri- a De- i Pa- tris.

A- men.

Collect

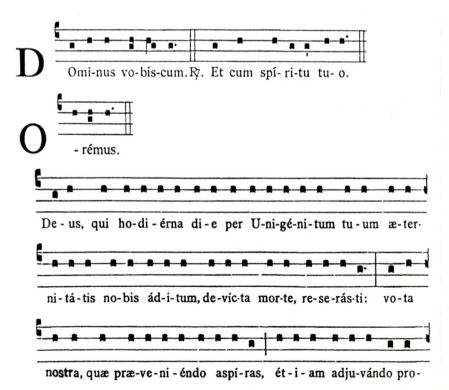

D Omi-nus vo-bís-cum. ℟. Et cum spí- ri-tu tu- o.

O - rémus.

De- us, qui ho-di- érna di- e per U-ni-gé-ni-tum tu- um æ-ter-

ni- tá-tis no-bis ád-i-tum, de-víc-ta mor-te, re-se-rás-ti: vo-ta

nostra, quæ præ-ve-ni- éndo aspí-ras, ét-i- am adju-vándo pro-

5

séque-re. Per e-ún-dem Dó-mi-num nostrum Je-sum Chris-tum,

Fí-li-um tu-um: Qui te-cum vi-vit et regnat in u-ni-tá-te

Spí-ri-tus Sanc-ti De-us, per óm-ni-a sǽ-cu-la sæ-cu-ló-rum.

℟. A-men.

men-to ma-li-ti-ae, et ne-qui-ti-ae: sed in a-zy-mis

sin-ce-ri-ta-tis, et ve-ri-ta-tis.

Epistle

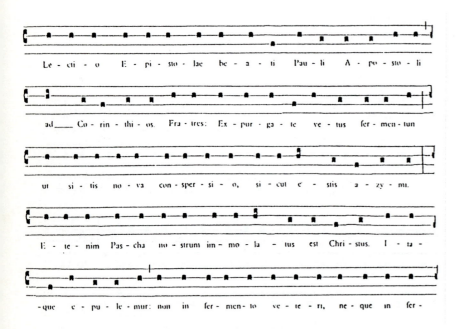

Lec-ti-o E-pi-sto-lae be-a-ti Pau-li A-po-sto-li

ad Co-rin-thi-os. Fra-tres: Ex-pur-ga-te ve-tus fer-men-tum

ut si-tis no-va con-sper-si-o, si-cut e-stis a-zy-mi.

E-te-nim Pas-cha no-strum im-mo-la-tus est Chri-stus. I-ta-

-que e-pu-le-mur: non in fer-men-to ve-te-ri, ne-que in fer-

Gradual

GR. II

Ps. 117, 24 et 1

H Aec di- es, • quam fe- cit

Dó- mi- nus: exsulté- mus,

et lae-té- mur in e- a.

℣. Confi-témi-ni Dó- mi- no,

quó- ni- am bo- nus:

quó-ni-am in saé- cu-lum

mi-se-ri-cór- di-a e-ius.

Alleluia

1 Cor. 5, 7

VII

A

L-le-lú- ia. * ij.

℣. Pascha no-strum immo-lá-

tus est *Chri- stus.

quid vi-dísti in vi- a? Sepúlcrum Christi vi-véntis, et gló-

ri- am vi-di re-surgéntis : Angé-li-cos testes, sudá-ri- um,

et vestes. Surré-xit Christus spes me- a : praecédet su-os in

Ga-li-laé- am. Scimus Christum surrexísse a mórtu- is ve-re :

tu no-bis, victor Rex, mi-se-ré-re. A- men. Al-le-lú-ja.

Sequence

SEQ. I

V

Ictimae paschá-li laudes * ímmo-lent Christi- á-ni.

Agnus re-démit oves : Christus ínno-cens Patri re-conci-

li- ávit pecca-tó-res. Mors et vi-ta du-él-lo confli-xé-re mi-rán-

do : dux vi-tae mórtu- us, regnat vivus. Dic no-bis Ma-rí- a,

Gospel

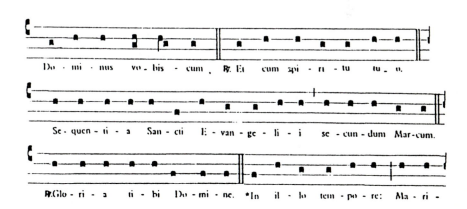

Do- mi- nus vo-bis - cum. ℟. Et cum spi- ri- tu tu- o.

Se- quen- ti- a Sancti E- van- ge- li - i se-cun-dum Mar-cum.

℟. Glo- ri - a ti - bi Do- mi- ne. *In il-lo tem-po- re: Ma-ri-

7

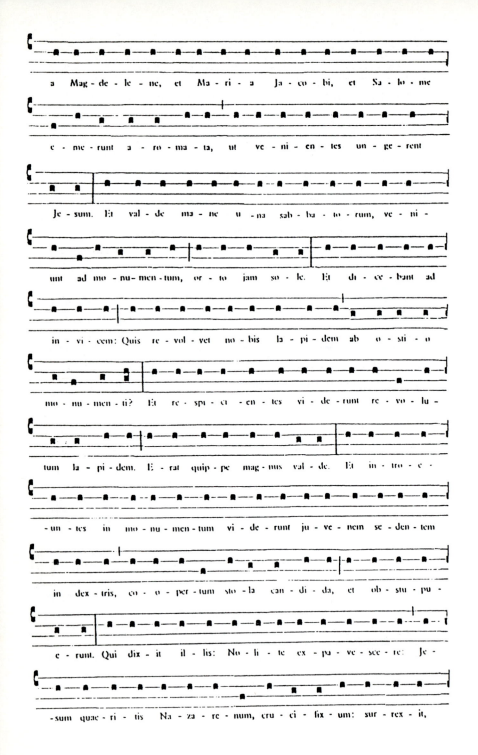

a Mag-de-le-ne, et Ma-ri-a Ja-co-bi, et Sa-lo-me

e-me-runt a-ro-ma-ta, ut ve-ni-en-tes un-ge-rent

Je-sum. Et val-de ma-ne u-na sab-ba-to-rum, ve-ni-

unt ad mo-nu-men-tum, or-to jam so-le. Et di-ce-bant ad

in-vi-cem: Quis re-vol-vet no-bis la-pi-dem ab o-sti-o

mo-nu-men-ti? Et re-spi-ci-en-tes vi-de-runt re-vo-lu-

tum la-pi-dem. E-rat quip-pe mag-nus val-de. Et in-tro-e-

un-tes in mo-nu-men-tum vi-de-runt ju-ve-nem se-den-tem

in dex-tris, co-o-per-tum sto-la can-di-da, et ob-stu-pu-

e-runt. Qui dix-it il-lis: No-li-te ex-pa-ve-sce-re: Je-

-sum quae-ri-tis Na-za-re-num, cru-ci-fix-um: sur-rex-it,

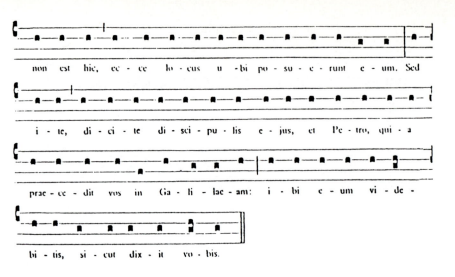

non est hic, ec-ce lo-cus u-bi po-su-e-runt e-um. Sed

i-te, di-ci-te di-sci-pu-lis e-jus, et Pe-tro, qui-a

prae-ce-dit vos in Ga-li-lae-am: i-bi e-um vi-de-

bi-tis, si-cut dix-it vo-bis.

Credo

XI. s.

IV

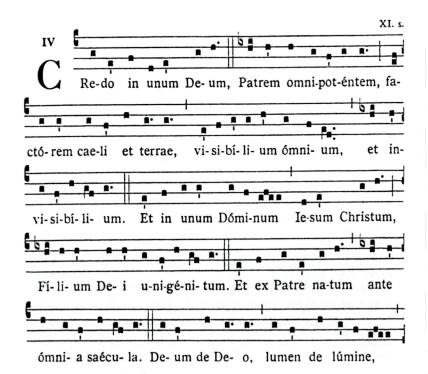

C Re-do in unum De-um, Patrem omni-pot-éntem, fa-

ctó-rem cae-li et terrae, vi-si-bí-li-um ómni-um, et in-

vi-si-bí-li-um. Et in unum Dómi-num Ie-sum Christum,

Fí-li-um De-i u-ni-gé-ni-tum. Et ex Patre na-tum ante

ómni-a saécu-la. De-um de De-o, lumen de lúmine,

De- um ve-rum de De- o ve-ro. Gé-ni-tum, non factum, consub-

stanti- á-lem Patri : per quem ómni- a facta sunt. Qui pro-

pter nos hómi-nes, et propter nostram sa-lú-tem descéndit de

cae-lis. Et incarná-tus est de Spí-ri-tu Sancto ex Ma-rí- a

Vírgi- ne : Et homo factus est. Cru-ci- fí-xus ét-i- am pro

no-bis : sub Pónti- o Pi- lá-to passus, et sepúl-tus est. Et

re-surréxit térti- a di- e, se-cúndum Scriptú-ras. Et ascén-

dit in caelum : se-det ad déxte-ram Patris. Et í-te-rum ven-

tú-rus est cum gló-ri- a, iu-di-cá-re vivos et mórtu- os :

cu-ius regni non e- rit fi- nis. Et in Spí- ri-tum Sanctum,

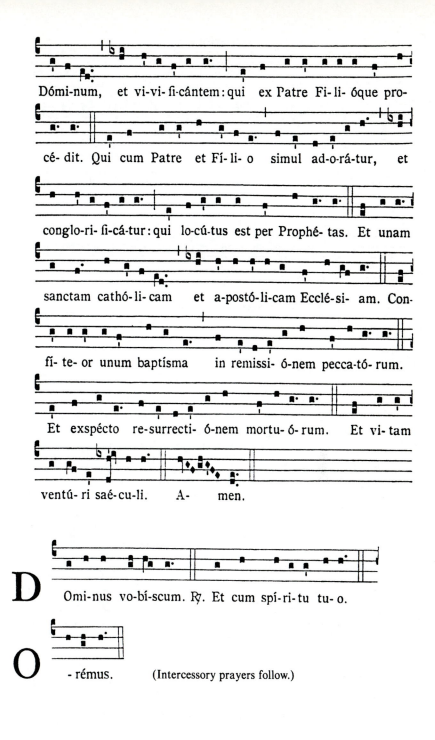

Dómi-num, et vi-vi- fi-cántem : qui ex Patre Fi- li- óque pro-

cé- dit. Qui cum Patre et Fí-li- o simul ad-o-rá-tur, et

conglo-ri- fi-cá-tur : qui lo-cú-tus est per Prophé- tas. Et unam

sanctam cathó-li- cam et a-postó-li-cam Ecclé-si- am. Con-

fi- te- or unum baptísma in remissi- ó-nem pecca-tó- rum.

Et exspécto re-surrecti- ó-nem mortu- ó- rum. Et vi- tam

ventú- ri saé-cu-li. A- men.

D
Omi-nus vo-bí-scum. ℞. Et cum spí-ri-tu tu- o.

O
- rémus. (Intercessory prayers follow.)

9

Offertory

Ps. 75, 9. 10

OF. IV

Terra *tré-mu- it, et qui- é- vit,

dum re-súrge- ret in iudí- ci- o De- us,

al- le- lú- ia.

Secret (spoken)

Suscipe, quaesumus Domine, preces populi tui
cum oblationibus hostiarum: ut paschalibus initiata
mysteriis, ad aeternitatis nobis medelam, te operante, proficiant. Per Dominum . . .

R̞ Amen.

Preface

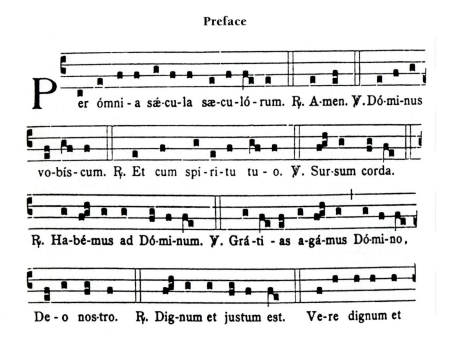

Per ómni- a sǽ-cu-la sæ-cu-ló- rum. R̞. A·men. V̞.Dó·mi-nus

vo-bís- cum. R̞. Et cum spi-ri-tu tu - o. V̞. Sur-sum corda.

R̞. Ha-bé-mus ad Dó-mi-num. V̞. Grá-ti - as a-gá-mus Dó-mi-no,

De - o nos-tro. R̞. Dig-num et justum est. Ve-re dignum et

justum est, æquum et sa-lu-tá-re: Te qui-dem, Dó-mi-ne, omni

tém-po-re, sed in hac po-tís-si-mum di - e glo-ri-ó-si-us

præ-di - cá-re, cum Páscha nostrum immo-lá-tus est Chris-tus.

Ipse e-nim ve-rus est Agnus, qui ábstu-lit pec-cá-ta mundi.

Qui mortem nostram mo-ri-éndo destrú-xit et vi - tam re-sur-

géndo re-pa-rá-vit. Et íd-e-o cum Ange-lis et Arch-ánge-lis,

cum Thro-nis et Do-mi-na-ti - ó-ni-bus cum-que omni mi-li-

ti - a cæ-lés-tis ex-ér-ci-tus hymnum gló-ri-æ tu - æ cá-ni-mus.

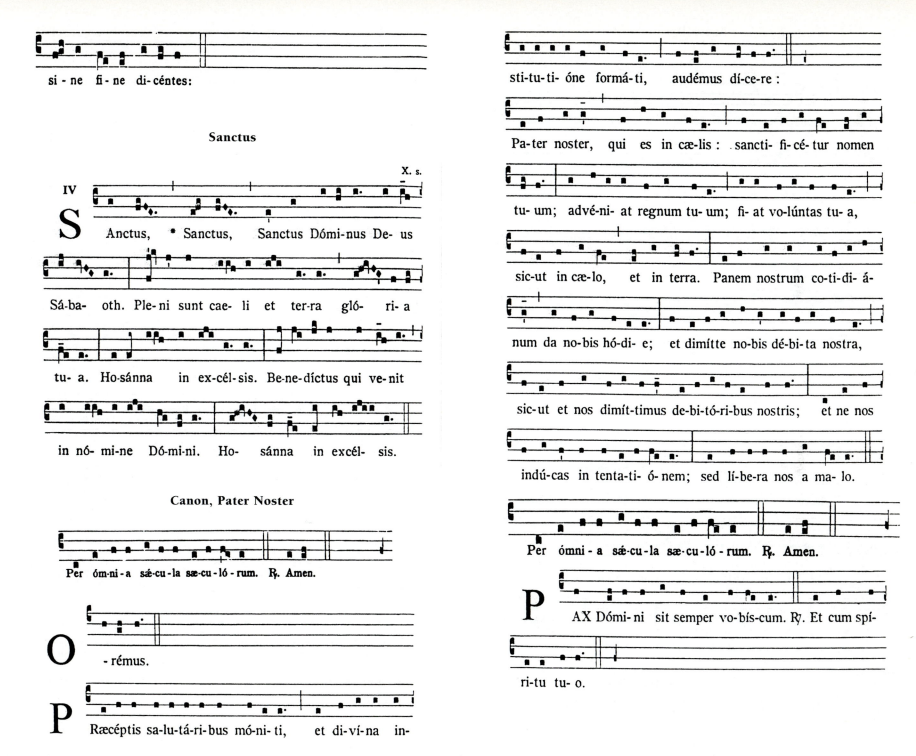

si - ne fi - ne di - céntes:

Sanctus

IV

SAnctus, * Sanctus, Sanctus Dómi-nus De- us
Sá-ba- oth. Ple-ni sunt cae- li et ter-ra gló- ri- a
tu- a. Ho-sánna in ex-cél-sis. Be-ne-díctus qui ve-nit
in nó- mi-ne Dó-mi-ni. Ho- sánna in excél- sis.

Canon, Pater Noster

Per óm-ni- a sǽ-cu -la sæ-cu-ló- rum. R̦. Amen.

O- rémus.

PRæcéptis sa-lu-tá-ri-bus mó-ni- ti, et di-ví-na in-

sti-tu-ti- óne formá- ti, audémus dí-ce-re :

Pa-ter noster, qui es in cæ-lis : sancti- fi-cé-tur nomen

tu- um; advé-ni- at regnum tu- um; fi- at vo-lúntas tu- a,

sic-ut in cæ-lo, et in terra. Panem nostrum co-ti-di- á-

num da no-bis hó-di- e; et dimítte no-bis dé-bi-ta nostra,

sic-ut et nos dimít-timus de-bi-tó-ri-bus nostris; et ne nos

indú-cas in tenta-ti- ó- nem; sed lí-be-ra nos a ma- lo.

Per ómni- a sǽ-cu -la sæ-cu-ló- rum. R̦. Amen.

PAX Dómi- ni sit semper vo-bís-cum. R̦. Et cum spí-

ri-tu tu- o.

Agnus Dei

IV   X. s.

A-gnus De- i, * qui tol-lis peccá- ta mun- di : mi-se-

ré- re no- bis.   Agnus De- i, * qui tol-lis peccá-

ta mun- di : mi-se-ré- re no- bis.   Agnus De- i, *

qui tol-lis peccá- ta mun- di : dona no- bis pa- cem.

Communion

CO. VI   1 Cor. 5, 7. 8

P Ascha nostrum * immo-lá- tus est Chri-

stus, alle-lú- ia : í-ta- que e-pu- lé- mur

in á- zy-mis since-ri-tá- tis et ve-ri-tá- tis, alle-

lú- ia, alle- lú- ia, al-le- lú- ia.

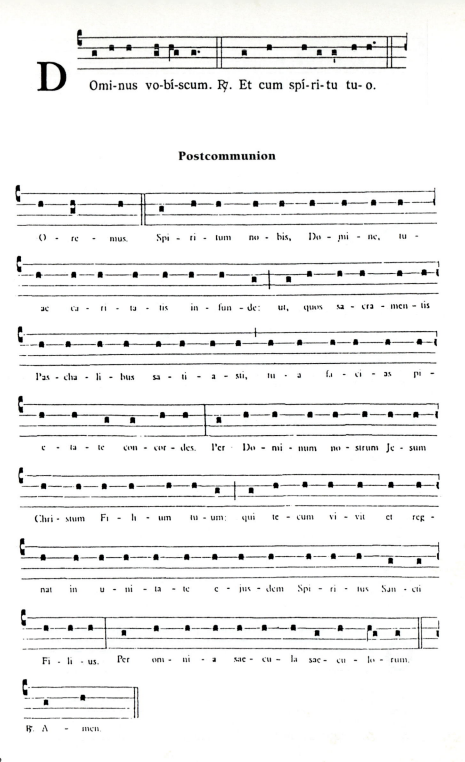

D Omi-nus vo-bí-scum. ℟. Et cum spí-ri-tu tu- o.

Postcommunion

O- re- mus. Spi- ri- tum no- bis, Do-mi- ne, tu-

ac ca- ri- ta- tis in-fun- de : ut, quos sa- cra- men- tis

Pas- cha- li- bus sa- ti- a- sti, tu- a fa- ci- as pi-

e- ta- te con- cor- des. Per Do- mi- num no- strum Je- sum

Chri- stum Fi- li- um tu- um : qui te- cum vi- vit et reg-

nat in u- ni- ta- te e- jus- dem Spi- ri- tus San- cti

Fi- li- us. Per om- ni- a sae- cu- la sae- cu- lo- rum.

℟. A- men.

Dismissal

VIII

D-Omi-nus vo-bí-scum. Ry. Et cum spí-ri-tu tu- o.

I- te, missa est, alle-lú- ia,   alle-   lú- ia.
De- o grá-ti- as, alle-lú- ia,   alle-   lú- ia.

INTROIT

Resurrexi, et adhuc tecum sum, alleluia:
posuisti super me manum tuam, alleluia:
mirabilis facta est scientia tua, alleluia, alleluia.

I have risen, and I am still with thee, alleluia:
thou hast laid thy hand upon me, alleluia:
thy knowledge has done wonderful things,
alleluia, alleluia.

Ps.
Domine probasti me, et cognovisti me:

tu cognovisti sessionem meam, et resurrectionem meam.

Gloria Patri et Filio, et Spiritui Sancto.

Sicut erat in principio, et nunc, et semper, et in saecula saeculorum.* Amen.

Psalm [138/139:1–2]
Lord, thou has proven me, and thou hast known me:

thou hast known my sitting down, and my rising up.

Glory be to the Father and to the Son, and to the Holy Spirit.

As it was in the beginning, and [is] now, and always [= and ever shall be], and through ages of ages.* Amen.

*sometimes translated as "world without end"

KYRIE

Kyrie eleison.
Christe eleison.
Kyrie eleison.

Lord have mercy.
Christ have mercy.
Lord have mercy.

GLORIA

Gloria in excelsis Deo.
Et in terra pax hominibus bonae voluntatis.
Laudamus te.
Benedicimus te.
Adoramus te.
Glorificamus te.
Gratias agimus tibi propter magnam gloriam tuam.
Domine Deus, Rex caelestis, Deus Pater omnipotens.
Domine Fili unigenite Jesu Christe.
Domine Deus, Agnus Dei, Filius Patris.

Glory to God in the highest.
And on earth peace to men of good will.
We praise thee.
We bless thee.
We adore thee.
We glorify thee.
We give thee thanks for thy great glory.

Lord God, King of heaven, God the Father almighty.
Lord, the only-begotten Son, Jesus Christ.
Lord God, Lamb of God, Son of the Father.

Qui tollis peccata mundi, miserere nobis.

Qui tollis peccata mundi, suscipe deprecationem nostram.
Qui sedes ad dexteram Patris, miserere nobis.

Quoniam tu solus sanctus.
Tu solus Dominus.
Tu solus Altissimus, Jesu Christe.
Cum Sancto Spiritu, in gloria Dei Patris.
Amen.

[Thou] Who takest away the sins of the world, have mercy on us.
[Thou] Who takest away the sins of the world, receive our prayer.
[Thou] Who sittest at the right hand of the Father, have mercy on us.
Because thou alone [art] holy.
Thou alone [art] Lord.
Thou alone [art] Most High, Jesus Christ.
With the Holy Spirit, in the glory of God the Father.
Amen.

COLLECT

Dominus vobiscum.
Ry. Et cum spiritu tuo.

The Lord be with you.
Ry. And with thy spirit.

Oremus.

Let us pray.

Deus, qui hodierna die per Unigenitum tuum, aeternitatis nobis aditum devicta morte reserasti:
vota nostra, quae praeveniendo aspiras, etiam adjuvando prosequere.
Per eundem Dominum nostrum Jesum Christum, Filium tuum:
Qui tecum vivet et regnat in unitate Spiritus Sancti Deus, per omnia saecula saeculorum.

Ry. Amen.

God, who this day through the only-begotten Son, conquered death, you have opened to us the gate of eternity [= everlasting life]:
help us attain [or, fulfill] our desires, which thou dost inspire.
Through the same Jesus Christ, our Lord, thy Son:
Who with thee lives and reigns God in the unity of the Holy Spirit, through all ages of ages [= for ever].
Ry. Amen.

EPISTLE (I Cor. 5:7–8)

Lectio Epistolae beati Pauli Apostoli ad Corinthios.

A reading from the Epistle of the blessed apostle Paul to the Corinthians.

Fratres: Expurgate vetus fermentu[m], ut sitis nova conspersio, sicut estis azymi. Etenim Pascha nostrum immolatus est Christus.

Itaque epulemur: non in fermento veteri, neque in fermento malitiae, et nequitiae: sed in azymis sinceritatis, et veritatis.

Brethren: Purge out the old leaven, so that you may be a new mixture [literally, temperament], as you are unleavened. For Christ, our Passover, has been sacrificed.

Therefore, let us feast: not with the old leaven, nor with the leaven of malice, and wickedness, but with the unleavened [bread] of sincerity, and truth.

GRADUAL

Haec dies, quam fecit Dominus: exsultemus, et laetemur in ea.
Ꝟ Confitemini Domino, quoniam bonus: quoniam in saeculum misericordia ejus.

This is the day which the Lord hath made: we will rejoice, and let us be glad in it.
Ꝟ Confess* to the Lord, for He is good: for His mercy [endures] for ever.

*Literally, confess; however, in the Bible the verse is variously translated as "Praise the Lord" and "Give thanks to the Lord." (Psalm 135/136:1)

ALLELUIA

Alleluia. (3 times)
Ꝟ Pascha nostrum immolatus est Christus.

Alleluia.
Ꝟ Christ, our Passover, has been sacrificed.

13

SEQUENCE

Victimae paschali laudes immolent Christiani.

Agnus redemit oves: Christus innocens Patri reconciliavit peccatores.
Mors et vita duello conflixere mirando: dux vitae mortuus, regnat vivus.

Dic nobis Maria, quid vidisti in via? Sepulchrum Christi viventis, et gloriam vidi resurgentis:
Angelicos testes, sudarium, et vestes. Surrexit Christus spes mea: praecedet suos in Galilaeam.
Scimus Christum surrexisse a mortuis vere: tu nobis, victor Rex, miserere.
Amen. Alleluia.

To the Paschal Victim let Christians offer songs of praise.

The Lamb has redeemed the sheep: sinless Christ has reconciled sinners to the Father.
Death and life have clashed in a miraculous combat: the leader of life died, [yet] living he reigns.

Tell us, Mary, what you saw on the way? I saw the tomb of the living Christ, and the glory of [His] resurrection:
The angel witnesses, the napkin, and the grave-clothes. Christ, my hope, has risen: he precedes his own into Galilee.
We know Christ has truly risen from the dead: Thou, victor King, have mercy on us.
Amen. Alleluia.

GOSPEL (Mark 16:1–7)

Dominus vobiscum.
R/ Et cum spiritu tuo.

Sequentia Sancti Evangelii secundum Marcum.
R/ Gloria tibi Domine.

In illo tempore:
Maria Magdalene, et Maria Jacobi, et Salome emerunt aromata, ut venientes ungerent Jesum.
Et valde mane una sabbatorum, veniunt ad monumentum, orto jam sole.
Et dicebant ad invicem: Quis revolvet nobis lapidem ab ostio monumenti?

Et respicientes viderunt revolutum lapidem.

Erat quippe magnus valde.
Et introeuntes in monumentum viderunt juvenem sedentem in dextris, coopertum stola candida, et obstupuerunt.

Qui dicit illis: Nolite expavescere: Jesum quaeritis Nazarenum, crucifixum: surrexit, non est hic, ecce locus ubi posuerunt eum.

Sed ite, dicite discipulis ejus, et Petro, quia praecedit vos in Galilaeam: ibi eum videbitis, sicut dixit vobis.

The Lord be with you.
R/ And with thy spirit.

Next, [reading] from the holy Gospel according to Mark.
R/ Glory to Thee, Lord.

At that time:
Mary Magdalene, and Mary [the mother] of James, and Salome bought spices, in order that they might come and anoint Jesus.
And very early in the morning on the first day of the week, they came to the tomb, at sunrise.
And they said to one another: Who will roll away for us the stone from the door of the sepulchre?
And, looking, they saw the stone [had been] rolled back.
Certainly, it was very large.
And entering the sepulchre, they saw a young man sitting on the right side, clothed in a long, dazzling white robe, and they were astonished.
He said to them: Do not be exceedingly frightened: You seek Jesus of Nazareth, [who was] crucified: He has risen; he is not here; behold the place where they laid him.
But go, tell his disciples, and Peter, he precedes you into Galilee: there you will see him, as he told you.

CREDO

Credo in unum Deum,
Patrem omnipotentem, factorem caeli et terrae, visibilium omnium, et invisibilium.
Et in unum Dominum Jesum Christum, Filium Dei unigenitum.
Et ex Patre natum ante omnia saecula.
Deum de Deo, lumen de lumine, Deum verum de Deo vero.
Genitum, non factum, consubstantialem Patri: per quem omnia facta sunt.
Qui propter nos homines, et propter nostram salutem descendit de caelis.
Et incarnatus est de Spiritu Sancto ex Maria Virgine: Et homo factus est.
Crucifixus etiam pro nobis: sub Pontio Pilato passus, et sepultus est.
Et resurrexit tertia die, secundum Scripturas.

Et ascendit in caelum: sedet ad dexteram Patris.
Et iterum venturus est cum gloria, judicare vivos et mortuos: cujus regni non erit finis.

Et in Spiritum Sanctum, Dominum, et vivificantem: qui ex Patre Filioque procedit.
Qui cum Patre et Filio simul adoratur, et conglorificatur: qui locutus est per Prophetas.

Et unam sanctam catholicam et apostolicam Ecclesiam.
Confiteor unum baptisma in remissionem peccatorum.
Et exspecto resurrectionem mortuorum. Et vittam venturi saeculi.
Amen.

I believe in one God,
The Father almighty, maker of heaven and earth, [and] of all things visible and invisible.
And in one Lord, Jesus Christ, only-begotten Son of God.
And born of the Father before all ages.
God from God, light from light, true God from true God.
Born, not made, of one substance with the Father: through whom all things were made.
Who for us men [i.e., mankind] and for our salvation came down from heaven.
And was made incarnate by the Holy Spirit of the Virgin Mary: And was made man.
Also, he was crucified for us: he suffered under Pontius Pilate and was buried.
And he rose again on the third day, according to the Scriptures.
And he ascended into heaven: he sits at the right hand of the Father.
And he will come again with glory, to judge the living and the dead: of his kingdom there will be no end.
And in the Holy Spirit, Lord, and giver of life: who proceeds from the Father and the Son.
Who, together with the Father and the Son, is worshiped and glorified: who spoke through the prophets.
And in one holy, universal, and apostolic church.
I confess* one baptism in remission of sins. [*or, I acknowledge one baptism. . . .]
And I look forward to the resurrection of the dead. And life in the ages to come.
Amen.

Dominus vobiscum.
R/ Et cum spiritu tuo.

Oremus.

The Lord be with you.
R/ And with thy spirit.

Let us pray. [Prayers follow.]

OFFERTORY (Ps. 75/76:9, 10)

Terra tremuit, et quievit, dum resurgeret in judicio Deus, alleluia.

The earth trembled, and was still, when God rose in judgment, alleluia.

SECRET

Suscipe, quaesumus Domine, preces populi tui cum oblationibus hostiarum:
ut paschalibus initiata mysteriis, ad aeternitatis nobis medelem, te operante, proficiant. Per Dominum . . .
R/ Amen.

Accept, we beseech thee, Lord, the prayers of thy people together with the sacrifice they offer:
that what has been begun by these Easter mysteries may, by thy working, profit us to everlasting salvation. Through our Lord . . .
R/ Amen.

PREFACE

Per omnia saecula saeculorum.
℟ Amen.
Dominus vobiscum.
℟ Et cum spiritu tuo.

Sursum corda.
℟ Habemus ad Dominum.

Gratias agamus Domino, Deo nostro.
℟ Dignum et justum est.

Vere dignum et justum est, aequum et salutare:
Te quidem, Domine, omni tempore, sed in hac potissimum die gloriosius praedicare: cum Pascha nostrum immolatus est Christus.
Ipse enim verus est Agnus, qui abstulit peccata mundi.
Qui mortem nostram moriendo destruxit et vitam resurgendo reparavit.
Et ideo cum Angelis et Archangelis, cum Thronis et Dominationibus cumque omni militia caelestis exercitus hymnum gloriae tuae canimus, sine fine dicentes:

SANCTUS

Sanctus, Sanctus, Sanctus Dominus Deus Sabaoth.
Pleni sunt caeli et terra gloria tua.
Hosanna in excelsis.
Benedictus qui venit in nomine Domini.
Hosanna in excelsis.

CANON, PATER NOSTER

Per omnia saecula saeculorum.
℟ Amen.

Oremus:

Praeceptis salutaribus moniti, et divina institutione formati, audemus dicere:
Pater noster, qui es in caelis:
sanctificetur nomen tuum:
adveniat regnum tuum;
fiat voluntas tua, sicut in caelo, et in terra.
Panem nostrum cotidianum da nobis hodie;
et dimitte nobis debita nostra, sicut et nos dimittimus debitoribus nostris;
et ne nos inducas in tentationem; sed libera nos a malo.

Per omnia saecula saeculorum.
℟ Amen.

For ever and ever. [or, Through all ages of ages.]
℟ Amen.
The Lord be with you.
℟ And with thy spirit.

Lift up your hearts.
℟ We have [lifted them up] to the Lord.

Let us give thanks to the Lord, our God.
℟ It is fitting and just.

It is truly fitting and just, right and profitable:
Indeed, to praise thee, Lord, at all times, but chiefly on this glorious day when Christ, our Passover, has been sacrificed for us.
For he is the true Lamb, who has taken away the sins of the world.
Who, dying, destroyed our death, and, rising again, he has restored [our] life.
And, therefore, with the angels and archangels, with thrones and dominations, and with all the array of the heavenly hosts, we sing a hymn to thy glory, unceasingly chanting:

Holy, Holy, Holy, Lord God of Sabaoth.
Heaven and earth are full of thy glory.
Hosanna in the highest.
Blessed [is he] who comes in the name of the Lord.
Hosanna in the highest.

For ever and ever. [or, Through all ages of ages.]
℟ Amen.

Let us pray:

Admonished by wholesome precepts, and patterned by divine instruction, we dare to say:
Our Father, who art in heaven:
hallowed be thy name:
thy kingdom come:
thy will be done, as in heaven, so on earth.
Give us today our daily bread;
and forgive us our debts [trespasses], as we forgive our debtors [those who trespass against us];
and lead us not into temptation; but deliver us from evil.

For ever and ever. [or, Through all ages of ages.]
℟ Amen.

Pax Domini sit semper vobiscum.
℟ Et cum spiritu tuo.

AGNUS DEI

Agnus Dei, qui tollis peccata mundi: miserere nobis.
Agnus Dei, qui tollis peccata mundi: miserere nobis.
Agnus Dei, qui tollis peccata mundi: dona nobis pacem.

COMMUNION

Pascha nostrum immolatus est Christus, alleluia:
itaque epulemur in azymis sinceritatis et veritatis,
alleluia, alleluia, alleluia.

Dominus vobiscum.
℟ Et cum spiritu tuo.

POSTCOMMUNION

Oremus.

Spiritum nobis, Domine, tuae caritatis infunde: ut, quos sacramentis Paschalibus satiasti, tua facias pietate concordes.

Per Dominum nostrum Jesum Christum Filium tuum: qui tecum vivit et regnat in unitate ejusdem Spiritus Sancti Filius.
Per omnia saecula saeculorum.
℟ Amen.

DISMISSAL

Dominus vobiscum.
℟ Et cum spiritu tuo.

Ite, missa est, alleluia, alleluia.

℟ Deo gratias, alleluia, alleluia.

The peace of the Lord be with you always.
℟ And with thy spirit.

Lamb of God, who takest away the sins of the world: have mercy on us.
Lamb of God, who takest away the sins of the world: have mercy on us.
Lamb of God, who takest away the sins of the world: give us peace.

Christ, our Passover, has been sacrificed, alleluia:
therefore, let us feast with the unleavened [bread] of sincerity and truth,
alleluia, alleluia, alleluia.

The Lord be with you.
℟ And with thy spirit.

Let us pray.

God, impart to us the spirit of your love: so that, [those] whom thou hast fed with the Paschal sacrament, may be brought into harmony by thy compassion.
Through our Lord, Jesus Christ, thy Son: who lives and reigns with you in the same unity of the Holy Spirit.
For ever and ever. [or, Through all ages of ages.]
℟ Amen.

The Lord be with you.
℟ And with thy spirit.

Go, it [the message] has been sent, alleluia, alleluia.
℟ Thanks be to God, alleluia, alleluia.

6 ABSOLVE, DOMINE, Tract
Anonymous

Tract. 8.

Absól- ve, * Dó-mi-ne, ánimas ómni-um fidé-li-um de-functó- rum ab ómni vín-cu-lo de-li- ctó- rum. ℣. Et grá-ti-a tú-a íllis succurrén- te, me-re-ántur e-váde-re ju-dí-ci-um ulti- ó- nis. ℣. Et lú-cis aetér-nae be-a-ti-tú- di- ne * pérfru- i.

Absolve, Domine, animas omnium fidelium defunctorum ab omni vinculo delictorum.

℣ Et gratia tua illis succurrente, mereantur evadere judicium ultionis.

℣ Et lucis aeternae beatitudine perfrui.

Lord, absolve [or, deliver] the souls of all of the faithful departed [deceased] from every bond of [their] sins.

℣ And, assisted in that by your grace, may they merit escaping [or, be able to escape] the judgment of punishment.

℣ And enjoy to the full the blessing of eternal light.

See DWM p. 46.

7 DIES IRAE, Sequence
Thomas of Celano (c. 1200–1250)

Seq. 1.

DI- es írae, dí-es ílla, Sólvet saéclum in favílla : Téste Dávid cum Sibýlla. Quántus trémor est futúrus, Quando jú-dex est ventúrus, Cúncta stricte discussúrus! Túba mí-rum spár-gens sónum Per sepúlcra regi-ónum, Cóget ómnes ante thrónum. Mors stupé-bit et natú-ra, Cum resúrget cre-a-túra, Judi-cán-ti responsúra. Líber scríptus pro-fe-ré-tur, In quo tó-tum continé-tur, Unde múndus judi-cé-tur. Júdex ergo cum sedébit, Quídquid lá-tet apparébit : Nil inúltum remanébit.

See DWM p. 46, 49.

Quid sum mí- ser tunc dictúrus? Quem patró- num roga-tú-

rus? Cum vix jústus sit secúrus. Rex treméndae ma-je-

stá-tis, Qui sal-vándos sálvas gra-tis, Sálva me, fons pi- e-

tá-tis. Recordá-re Jé- su pí- e, Quod sum cáusa tú-ae

ví-ae : Ne me pér-das illa dí- e. Quaérens me, se- dí-

sti lássus : Redemísti crúcem pássus : Tántus lá- bor non

sit cássus. Júste júdex ul-ti- ónis, Dó-num fac remissi-ó-

nis, Ante dí- em ra-ti- ónis. Ingemísco, tamquam

ré-us : Cúlpa rúbet vúltus mé- us : Suppli-cánti párce

Dé- us. Qui Ma-rí- am absolvísti, Et latró-nem exau-

dísti, Mí-hi quoque spem dedísti. Préces mé-ae non sunt

dígnae : Sed tu bó-nus fac benígne, Ne per-énni crémer

ígne. Inter óves ló- cum praésta, Et ab haédis me

sequéstra, Stá-tu-ens in párte déxtra. Confu-tá-tis ma-

ledíctis, Flámmis ácribus addíctis, Vóca me cum be-

nedíctis. Oro súpplex et acclí-nis, Cor contrí-tum qua-

si cí-nis : Gé-re cúram mé- i fí-nis. Lacrimósa dí- es

ílla, Qua resúrget ex favílla Judi-cándus hó- mo

ré-us : Hú- ic ergo pár- ce Dé-us. Pí- e Jésu Dómine,

dóna é- is réqui- em. A- men.

Dies irae, dies illa,
Solvet saeclum in favilla:
Teste David cum Sibylla.

Day of wrath, that day
the world comes to an end in glowing ashes:
attested [i.e., prophesied] by David and the Sibyl.

Quantus tremor est futurus,
Quando judex est venturus,
Cuncta stricte discussurus!

How great the trembling will be,
when the judge arrives,
[who] will put an end to all things by strict letter of the law!

Tuba mirum spargens sonum
Per sepulcra regionum,
Coget omnes ante thronum.

The war-trumpet pouring forth wondrous sound
through the tombs of the region,
will gather all [or, everything] before the throne.

Mors stupebit et natura,
Cum resurget creatura,
Judicanti responsura.

Death and Nature will be astonished,
when [all] creation rises again,
Responding for judgment.

Liber scriptus proferetur,
In quo totum continetur,
Unde mundus judicetur.

A written book will be brought forth,
in which everything will be contained,
from which the world will be judged.

Judex ergo cum sedebit,
Quidquid latet apparebit:
Nil inultum remanebit.

Then, when the judge is seated,
whatever is hidden will be made manifest:
nothing will remain unavenged.

Quid sum miser tunc dicturus?
Quem patronum rogaturus?
Cum vix justus sit securus.

What shall a wretch such as I say then?
Of what patron shall I ask help,
when the just [or, righteous] are scarcely secure?

Rex tremendae majestatis,
Qui salvandos salvas gratis,
Salva me, fons pietatis.

King of fearful [or, awe-inspiring] majesty,
who freely saves the redeemed,
save me, [O] fountain of mercy. [literally, respected source]

Recordare, Jesu pie,
Quod sum causa tuae viae:

Ne me perdas illa die.

Remember, holy Jesus,
that I am the cause of your course of action [i.e., your life on earth]:
Do not forsake me on that day.

Quaerens me, sedisti lassus:
Redemisti crucem passus:

Tantus labor non sit cassus.

Seeking me, you have sat down, weary:
Outstretched on the cross, you have ransomed [me]:
Let not such effort be in vain.

Juste judex ultionis,
Donum fac remissionis,
Ante diem rationis.

Just avenging judge,
make the gift of remission,
before the day of reckoning.

Ingemisco, tamquam reus:
Culpa rubet vultus meus:
Supplicanti parce, Deus.

I groan, as such a defendant [or, one accused]:
My countenance reddens with guilt:
[O] God, spare the suppliant [or, the one earnestly entreating].

Qui Mariam absolvisti,
Et latronem exaudisti,
Mihi quoque spem dedisti.

[You] Who have absolved Mary,
and have listened to the thief,
have given me hope, also.

Preces meae non sunt dignae:
Sed tu bonus fac benigne,
Ne perenni cremer igne.

My prayers are not worthy:
But You [who are] good, act benevolently
not to consume [my soul] in eternal fire.

Inter oves locum praesta,
Et ab haedis me sequestra,
Statuens in parte dextra.

Offer me a place among the sheep,
and sequester me from the goats,
causing me to stand in the portion at your right hand.

Confutatis maledictis,
Flammis acribus addictis,
Voca me cum benedictis.

The evil ones having been repressed,
doomed to bitter flames,
call me with the blessed.

Oro supplex et acclinis,
Cor contritum quasi cinis:
Gere curam mei finis.

I pray, suppliant, and kneeling,
heart contrite, as if in ashes:
Bear in Your care my ending.

Lacrimosa dies illa,
Qua resurget ex favilla
Judicandus homo reus:
Huic ergo parce Deus.

That sorrowful day,
when from the ashes mankind will rise again
bound for judgment:
Then, God, spare him.

Pie Jesu Domine,
dona eis requiem.

Merciful Lord Jesus,
give them rest.

Amen.

Amen.

8 Ecce Pater–Resurrexi, Troped Introit of Easter Mass

Anonymous

Ec - ce pa - ter cun - ctis ut ius - se - rat or - do per - ac - tis. Re -

sur - re - xi * et ad - huc te - cum sum al - le - lu - ia. Vic - tor ut

ad cae - los cal - ca - ta mor - te re - di - rem. Po - su - i - sti su - per

me ma - num tu - am al - le - lu - ia. Quo ge - nus hu - ma - num pul -

sis er - ro - ri - bus al - tum scan - de - - - - ret ad ce - lum. Mi - ra -

bi - lis fac - ta est sci - en - ti - a tu - a al - le - lu - ia al - le - lu - ia.

Ecce pater cunctis ut iusserat ordo peractis.	Behold, Father, all has been accomplished as it was commanded.
Resurrexi et adhuc tecum sum alleluia:	I have risen, and I am now with thee, alleluia:
Victor ut ad caelos calcata morte redirem.	So that, a victor, I might return to heaven from crushing death.
Posuisti super me manum tuam alleluia:	Thou hast laid thy hand upon me, alleluia:
Quo genus humanum pulsis erroribus altum scanderet ad celum.	So that humankind might rise to high heaven from its errant course.
Mirabilis facta est scientia tua alleluia alleluia.	Thy knowledge has done marvelous things, alleluia, alleluia.

Source: MS F–Pn Lat. 1121, fols. 11v–12.

See DWM p. 50.

9   QUEM QUAERITIS IN SEPULCHRO?

Anonymous

ANGEL
Quem quae - ri - tis in se-pul-chro, _ O _ Chris-ti - co - lae?

THREE WOMEN ... ANGEL
Je - sum Na-za-re-num cru-ci-fi - xum, _ O _ coe - li - co-la. Non est hic, ___

THREE WOMEN
sur-re-xit sic-ut pre-di - xe - rat; i - te, nun-ti-a - te qui-a sur - re - xit, di-cen-tes:

THREE WOMEN
Al - le-lu - ia, re-sur-re-xit _ Do-mi - nus _ ho-di - e, le-o for - tis, _

Chris-tus fi - li - us ___ De - i, De-o _ gra-ti - as, di - ci-te ___ ei - a!

ANGEL
Ve-ni-te _ et vi-de-te lo - cum u-bi po-si-tus e-rat Do-mi-nus, _ Al - le-lu-ia, _ al - le-lu-ia.

Ci-to e - un - tes, di-ci-te di-sci-pu-lis qui-a sur-re-xit Do-mi-nus. _ Al - le-lu-ia, _ al - le-lu-ia.

THREE WOMEN
Sur-re - xit Do-mi-nus de se-pul-chro, qui pro no - bis _ pe-pend-it in li - gno. Al - le - lu - ia.

ANGEL
Quem quaeritis in sepulchro, O Christicolae?

THREE WOMEN
Jesum Nazarenum crucifixum, O coelicola.

ANGEL
Whom do you seek in the sepulchre, O followers of Christ?

THREE WOMEN
Jeus of Nazareth, [who was] crucified, O celestial one.

See DWM pp. 50, 51, and Fig. 4.7.

ANGEL
Non est hic, surrexit sicut predixerat; ite, nun-
tiate quia surrexit, dicentes:

WOMEN
Alleluia, resurrexit Dominus hodie, leo fortis,
Christus filius Dei, Deo gratias, dicite eia!

ANGEL
Venite et videte locum ubi positus erat
Dominus, Alleluia, alleluia. Cito euntes,
dicite discipulis quia surrexit Dominus.
Alleluia, alleluia.

WOMEN
Surrexit Dominus de sepulchro, qui pro nobis
pependit in ligno. Alleluia.

ANGEL
He is not here, he is risen as he predicted; go,
announce that he is risen, saying:

WOMEN
Alleluia, the Lord is risen today, the strong
lion, Christ the son of God, thanks be to
God, say "Eia!"

ANGEL
Come and see the place where the Lord was
laid! Alleluia, alleluia. Go quickly, tell the
disciples that the Lord is risen. Alleluia,
alleluia.

WOMEN
The Lord is risen from the sepulchre, who for
us hung on the cross. Alleluia.

10   UT QUEANT LAXIS

Guido d'Arezzo (c. 990–1050)

Hymn. 2.
UT qué-ant láxis re-soná-re fíbris Mí- ra gestó-
rum fámu-li tu-ó-rum, Sól-ve pollú-ti lábi-i re-á-tum,
Sáncte Jo-ánnes.

Ut queant laxis resonare fibris
Mira gestorum famuli tuorum,
Solve polluti labii reatum,
Sancte Johannes.

So that the wonders of your deeds [while] in
servitude are able to resound,
Be acquitted of the accusation of depraved lips,
Saint John.

—attributed to Paul Diacré (c. 730–c. 799)

See DWM p. 59.

11 EARLY ORGANUM, Examples from ninth-century treatise

Musica enchiriadis

Anonymous

a TU PATRIS SEMPITERNUS ES FILIUS, Strict simple organum

Tu Patris sempiternus es Filius.
You are the ever-lasting Son of the Father.

See DWM p. 64.

b TU PATRIS SEMPITERNUS ES FILIUS, Strict composite organum

Tu Patris sempiternus es Filius.   You are the everlasting Son of the Father.

—from the *Te Deum laudamus.*

See DWM p. 64

c REX CAELI, Modified parallel organum

1. Rex cae-li, Do-mi-ne ma-ris un-di-so-ni
   Ti-ta-nis ni-ti-di squa-li-di-que so-li,
2. Te hu-mi-les fa-mu-li mo-du-lis ve-ne-ran-do pi-is
   Se ju-be-as fla-gi-tant va-ri-is li-be-ra-re ma-lis.

Rex caeli, Domine maris undisoni   King of heaven, Lord of the roaring sea,
Titanis nitidi squalidique soli,   of the dark earth and the shining sun,
Te humiles famuli modulis venerando   Your humble servants by worshiping
  piis   with pious phrases,
Se jubeas flagitant variis liberare malis.   Entreat You to free them, by Your
    command, from [their] various ills.

See DWM p. 65.

12 FREE ORGANUM

ALLELUIA, JUSTUS UT PALMA, from Anonymous treatise

Ad organum faciendum (c. 1100)

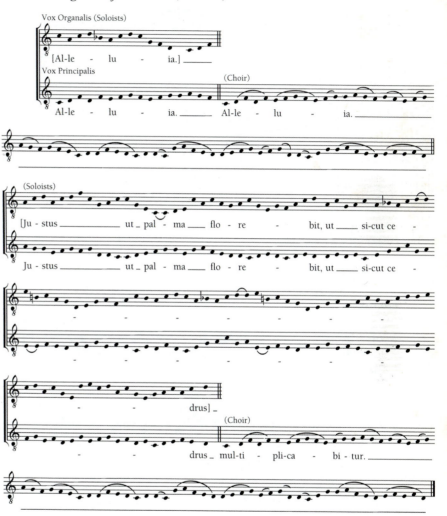

Alleluia.   Alleluia.
Justus ut palma florebit,   The righteous shall flourish like the palm tree:
ut sicut cedrus multiplicabitur.   he shall grow like a cedar.
Alleluia.   Alleluia.
  —Bible, Vulgate, Psalm 91:13

Transcribed from *Ad organum faciendum*, MS 17, Bib. Ambrosiana, Milan.

See DWM p. 67.

13 BENEDICAMUS [DOMINO], St. Martial Style organum

Anonymous

Benedicamus [Domino]   Let us bless [the Lord]

Transcribed from MS Lat. 1139, fol. 41

See DWM p. 68.

14 ALLELUIA, PASCHA NOSTRUM

a   Chant

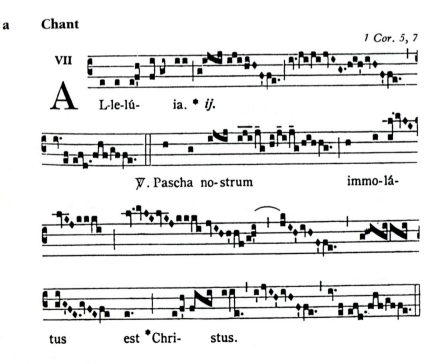

See DWM pp. 69, 78, and Fig. 5.16.

b   Chant with Discant-style Organum duplum and Clausulae

Léonin (fl. c. 1163–1190)

Transcribed from MS Pluteus 29.1, fol. 109

See DWM p. 69, and Fig. 5.16.

No - - strum.

No - - strum.

la -

[strum]

im - - - mo -

tus

-[a]

15   NOSTRA PHALANS, Versus

Ato

Nos - tra pha - lans plau - dat le - ta __ hac in di - e,

qua ath - le - ta Cris - ti gau - det si - ne __ me - ta, __ Ja - co - bus __ in

glo - ri - a. An - ge - lo - rum in __ cu - ri - a.

* ♪♪♪♪

Nostra phalans plaudat leta
hac in die, qua athleta
Cristi gaudet sine meta,
Jacobus in gloria.
Angelorum in curia.

Quem Herodes decollavit
et id circo coronavit
illum Christus et ditavit
in celesti patria.
Angelorum in curia.

Cuius corpus tumulatur
et a multis visitatur
et per illud eis datur
salus in Gallecia.
Angelorum in curia.

Ergo festum celebrantes
eius melos decantantes
persolvamus venerantes
dulces laudes Domino.
Angelorum in curia.

Let our joyful phalanx [or, company] praise
on this day, when the athlete
of Christ rejoices without limit,
James in glory.
In the court of the angels.

Whom Herod beheaded
and for that reason Christ crowned
him and endowed [or, enriched] him
in the celestial homeland.
In the court of the angels.

Whose body is buried
and is visited by many
and, for that, salvation is given
to them in Galicia.
In the court of the angels.

Therefore, celebrating his feast,
chanting [or, discanting] melodies,
venerating, let us offer*
sweet praises to the Lord.
In the court of the angels.

*persolvere = to offer as in payment
   or fulfillment of a vow

Transcribed from MS Cod. Calixtinus, fol. 185
See DWM p. 69, and Fig. 5.17.

16 CONGAUDEANT CATHOLICI, Conductus

Albertus

Con - gau - de - ant ca - tho - li - ci, le - ten - tur_ ci - ves

ce - li - ci di - e i - - -

- - - - - - sta.

* ♫♫♫

Congaudeant catholici,	Let catholics rejoice together,
letentur cives celici	let the citizens of heaven be glad
die ista.	on this day.
Clerus pulcris carminibus	Let the clergy devote itself
studeat atque cantibus,	to beautiful songs and chants,
die ista.	on this day.
Hec est dies laudabilis	This is the praiseworthy day,
divina luce nobilis,	the celebrated divine day,
die ista.	on this day.
Qua Jacobus palacia	Inasmuch as James ascended
ascendit ad celestia	from the palace into heaven
die ista.	on this day.
Vincens Herodis gladium	Herod's sword overcoming [him; i.e., James],
accepit vite bravium	he received the reward of eternal life
die ista.	on this day.
Ergo carenti termino,	Therefore, without ceasing,
benedicamus domino,	let us bless the Lord,
die ista.	on this day.
Magno patri familias	To the great Father of all
solvamus laudis gracias,	let us offer thanks of praise,
die ista.	on this day.

Transcribed from MS Cod. Calixtinus, fol. 185
See DWM p. 70, and Fig. 5.17.

17 REGNAT, Substitute Clausulae

Anonymous

18 ALLELUIA, NATIVITAS, Organum triplum

Pérotin (fl. c. 1190–c. 1225)

17a. Transcribed from MS Pluteus 29.1, fol. 168

See DWM p. 78.

See DWM p. 79, and Fig. 6.8.

19 MORS, Organum quadruplum

Pérotin (fl. c. 1190–c. 1225)

Alleluya.

℣ Nativitas gloriose Virginis Marie
ex semine Abra[h]e orta de tribu Iuda.

Alleluia.

℣ The birth of the glorious Virgin Mary,
from the seed of Abraham, risen from
the tribe of Judah.

Source: MS Pluteus 29.1.

See DWM pp. 79, 81.

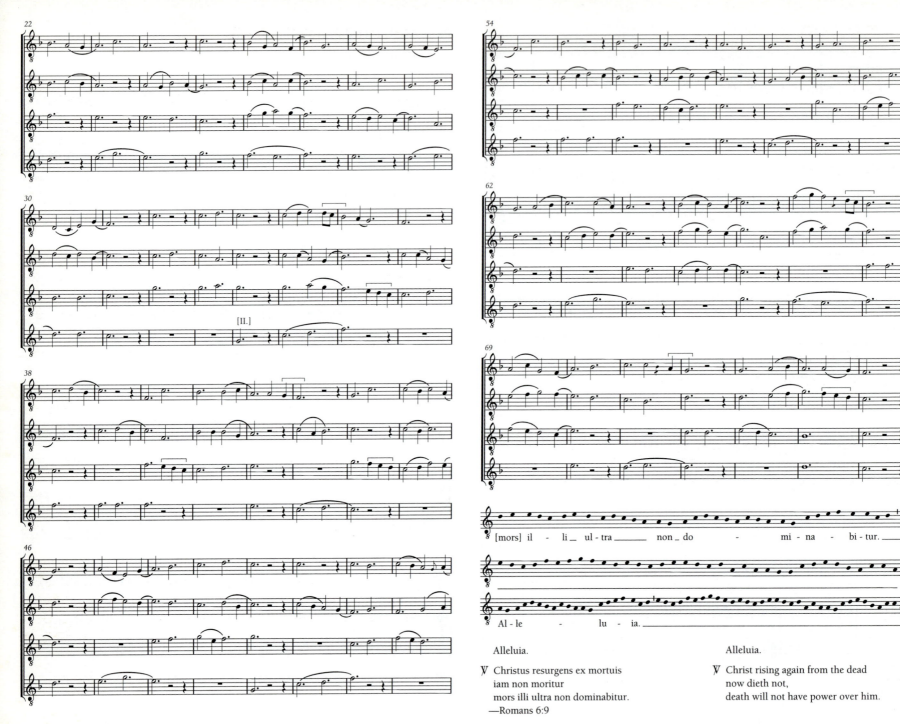

Alleluia.

℣ Christus resurgens ex mortuis
iam non moritur
mors illi ultra non dominabitur.
—Romans 6:9

Alleluia.

℣ Christ rising again from the dead
now dieth not,
death will not have power over him.

Alleluia.

20 VERI FLORIS, Conductus

Anonymous

Veri floris sub figura,
Quem produxit radix pura,
cleri nostri pia cura,
florem fecit mysticum
praeter usum laicum,
sensum trahens tropicum
floris a natura.

Under the figure of the true flower
which the pure root produced,
the loving devotion of our clergy
has made a mystical flower,
extracting an allegorical meaning,
beyond ordinary usage,
from the nature of a flower.

See DWM p. 82.

21 HAC IN ANNI IANUA, Conductus

Anonymous

Transcribed from MS W₁, fol. 78r.

See DWM p. 82.

Hac in anni ianua,	At this opening of [or, gateway to] the year,

Hac in anni ianua,
hoc in Ianuario,
tendamus ad ardua
virtutum subsidio.
Gaudia sunt mutua,
muto facto vitio.
Reproborum fatua
reprobatur actio.

At this opening of [or, gateway to] the year,
in this January,
let us direct our course toward heaven*
supported by virtue.
The joys are mutual,
vice has been made mute.
The foolish action of reprobates
is condemned.

*The line has double meaning, stating also, let
us turn to difficult tasks.

Anni novi novitas
nova leges afferens,
sequi vetat vetitas,
vetustatem auferens.
Probos probet probitas,
probis proba conferens.
Conteratur pravitas,
probitatem conterens.

The newness of the new year
bringing new laws,
it follows that it vetoes that which was prohibited,
sweeping away old conditions.
Moral integrity examines the evidence,
conferring approval on that which is good.
Let the wicked deeds [or, corrupt practices]
wearing down moral integrity be wiped out.

O felices nuptiae!
O felix humanitas,
cui nubit hodie
filii divinitas,
hinc divine glorie
non decrescit quantitas,
sed ad gradum gratie
nostra crescit parvitas.

O, blessed nuptials!
O, fortunate humanity,
to whom today
the divine Son is joined,
from now on, the magnitude of divine glory
does not decrease,
but to the degree of our grace
our significance increases [our smallness grows].

Nostris lumen tenebris
dat lumen de lumine,
prime culpe funebris
exclusa caligine.
De luce lux celebris
nascitur de virgine,
non carnis illecebris,
sed divino flamine.

The light of lights gives
sight [light] to our blindness [darkness],
having blotted out the darkness
of deadly original sin.
The celebrated light of light
is born of a virgin,
not by carnal seduction,
but by the Holy Spirit [by divine breath].

Carnis circumcisio,
mysterii vacua,
non fuit in filio
par quam nobis congrua
datur demonstratio
tollere superflua,
circumcisio vitio,
hac in anni ianua.

Circumcision of the flesh,
empty of mystery,
was not in the Son
by which fitting example
was given to us
to remove the excess,
pruning away evil,
at this beginning of the year.

22 EN NON DIU—QUANT VOI—EIUS IN ORIENTE, Motet

Anonymous

Transcribed from Montpellier MS H196, fols. 145v–146r.

See DWM pp. 83, 84, 111.

ner Et cha-piau de fleurs por-ter, Por si bele a-mi-e,
Et ser-vir et ho-ne-rer, Qui en joi-e veut du-rer.

Quant voi la rose es-pa-ni-e, L'her-be vert et le tans cler.
En non Diu, que que nus die, Au cuer me tient li maus d'a-mer!

TRIPLUM:

En non Diu, que que nus die,	In the name of God, whatever anyone says,
Quant voi l'herbe vert et le tans cler,	When I see the green grass and the clear skies
Et le rosignol chanter,	And the nightingale singing,
A donc fine amors me prie	Then true love begs me
Docement d'une joliveté chanter:	Sweetly to sing joyfully:
"Marions leisse Robim por moi amer!"	"Marion, leave Robin for my love!"
Bien me doi adés pener	Indeed I must take pains
Et chapiau de fleurs porter,	To wear a chaplet of flowers
Por si bele amie,	For such a beautiful lover,
Quant voi la rose espanie,	When I see the rose blooming,
L'herbe vert et le tans cler.	The green grass, and the clear skies.

DUPLUM:

Quant voi la rose espanie,	When I see the rose blooming,
L'herbe vert et le tans cler,	The green grass, and the clear skies,
Et le rosignol chanter,	And the nightingale singing,
A donc fine amors m'envie	Then true love inspires me
De joie fere et mener,	To be joyful and to pursue,
Car qui n'aime, il ne vit mie;	Because whoever does not love, only half lives;
Por ce se doit on pener:	Whoever wants joy to last
D'avoir amors a amie	Must take pains
Et servir et honerer,	To have Love for a friend
Qui en joie veut durer.	And to serve and honor her.
En non Diu, que que nus die,	In the name of God, whatever anyone says,
Au cuer mi tient li maus d'amer!	The pangs of love hold my heart!

TENOR:

Eius in oriente	From the east they . . .

23   PUCELETE—JE LANGUIS—DOMINO, Motet

Anonymous

Triplum: Pu-ce-le-te bele et a-ve-nant, jo-li-e-te, po-lie et plei-sant, la sa-de-te, que je de-sir tant, mi fait liés, jo-lis, en-voi-siés et a-mant: N'est en mai ein-si gai rous-si-gno-let chan-tant. S'a-me-rai de cuer en-tie-re-mant m'a-mi-e-te, la bru-ne-te, jo-li-e-te-ment. Bele a-mi-e, qui ma vie en

Duplum: Je lan-g[ui] des maus d'a-mours; Mieuz aim as-sez, qu'il m'o-ci-e que nul au-tre maus; trop est jo-li-e la mort. A-le-giés moi, douce a-mi-e, ces-te ma-la-

Tenor: Domino

See DWM p. 86.

vo bail-lie a -vés te-nu-e ___ tant, je voz cri mer-ci en sous-pi-rant.

di - e, qu'a-mours ne m'o - ci - e.

TRIPLUM:	TRIPLUM:
Pucelete	A little maid,
bele et avenant,	comely and fair,
joliete,	so pretty,
polie et pleisant,	graceful and pleasing,
la sadete,	the charming little one,
que je desir tant,	whom I desire so much,
mi fait liés,	makes me happy,
jolis, envoisiés	joyful, lighthearted
et amant:	and loving;
N'est en mai	A nightingale
einsi gai	singing in May
roussignolet chantant.	is not so gay.
S'amerai	I will love
de cuer entieremant	my little dark-haired
m'amiete,	sweetheart,
la brunete,	joyfully,
jolietement.	with my whole heart.
Bele amie,	Fair sweetheart,
qui ma vie	you who have
en vo baillie	so long had my life
avés tenue tant,	in your power,
je voz cri	sighing,
merci	I cry out to you
en souspirant.	for mercy.

DUPLUM:	DUPLUM:
Je lang[ui] des maus d'amours:	I languish with the pain of love:
Mieuz aim assez, qu'il m'ocie	I prefer that it, rather than
que nul autre maus;	any other malady, kill me;
trop est jolie la mort.	death is so sweet.
Alegiés moi, douce amie,	Relieve this illness,
ceste maladie,	sweet beloved,
qu'amours ne m'ocie.	so that love does not kill me.

TENOR:	TENOR:
Domino	Lord
—Anonymous	—Susan Stakel and Joel Reliken

24   AUCUNS VONT SOUVENT—AMOR QUI COR—KYRIE, Motet

Petrus de Cruce (fl. c. 1270–1300)

Triplum: Au - cuns vont sou - vent par leur en - vi - e mes-di-sant d'a-mours, mes il

Duplum: A - mor, ___ qui ___ cor ___

Tenor: Kyrie eleyson

n'est si bon-ne vi-e com d'a-mer loi - au - ment; quar _ d'a-mours vient

vul - ne — rat hu - ma - num, quem _

tou-te cour-toi-sie et tout ho-nour et tout bon en - se - gne - ment. Tout ce puet en li

ge - ne - rat car-na — lis af - fec-ti - o,

prou-ver, que a - mi - e veut fai-re sans bois-die et a-mer vrai-e - ment, que ja en li n'iert as-

num - quam ___ si - ne vi - ci - o vel ra - ro po -

Source: Montpellier MS H196, fols. 290v–291r.

See DWM p. 87, and Fig. 6.16.

TRIPLUM:

Aucuns vont souvent
par leur envie mesdisant
d'amours, mes il n'est si bonne vie
com d'amer loiaument;
quar d'amours vient toute courtoisie
et tout honour et tout bon ensegnement.
Tout ce puet en li prouver, qui amie
veut faire sans boisdie
et amer vraiement,
que ja en li n'iert assise vilanie
ne couvoitise d'amasser argent.
Ains aime bonne compaignie
et despent adés largement;
et si n'a en li felonnie
n'envie sus autre gent,
mes a chascun s'umelie
et parole courtoisement.
S'il a du tout sans partie
mis son cuer en amer entierement;
et sachiés, qu'il n'aime mie,
ains ment, s'il se demaine autrement.

DUPLUM:

Amor, qui cor vulnerat
humanum, quem generat
carnalis affectio,
numquam sine vicio
vel raro potest esse,
quoniam est necesse,
ut quo plus diligitur
res, que cito labitur
et transit, eominus
diligatur *Dominus*.

TENOR:

Kyrie eleyson

TRIPLUM:

Some often go around
badmouthing love out of envy,
but there is no life as good
as loving loyally;
for from love comes all courtesy
and all honor and all good upbringing.
All of this can be shown by one who
takes a sweetheart without deceit
and loves her truly.
Villainy will never reside in him,
nor will the desire to amass money.
Rather, he loves fair company
and always spends his money generously;
and there is in him no ill will
nor envy toward other people,
but he humbles himself
and speaks courteously toward other people.
If he has wholly, without exception,
set his heart entirely on loving;
and know that he who conducts himself other-
wise
does not love at all; rather he lies.

DUPLUM:

Love, which wounds the human heart,
love, which carnal lust
creates,
never or rarely can exist
without sin,
for it must be,
that the more a thing is loved,
which quickly decays
and passes away, the less
the Lord is loved.

TENOR:

Lord have mercy

35

25 SUMER IS ICUMEN IN, Rota-Motet

Anonymous

Transcribed from MS Harley 978, fol. 11v, British Museum

See DWM p. 89, and Plate 5.

The manuscript's performance instructions contain no directive for concluding this piece.

ENGLISH TEXT:

Sumer is icumen in,
Lhude sing cuccu.
Groweth sed and bloweth med,
And springth the wde nu.
Sing cuccu.
Awe bleteth after lomb,
Lhouth after calve cu;
Bulluc sterteth,
bucke verteth.
Murie sing cuccu.
Cuccu, cuccu.
Wel singes thu cuccu.
Ne swik thu naver nu.

LATIN TEXT:

Perspice Christicola, que dignatio.
Celicus agricola pro vitis vicio,
Filio non partens exposuit mortis exitio.

Qui captivos semivivos a supplicio
Vite, donat, et secum, coronat, in celi solio.

PES:

Sing cuccu nu, Sing cuccu.

Sing cuccu, Sing cuccu nu.

ENGLISH TEXT:

Summer is a-coming in,
Loudly sing cuckoo.
Groweth seed and bloweth mead,
And springeth the wood anew.
Sing cuckoo.
The ewe bleats for the lamb,
The cow lows for the calf;
The bullock leaps,
the buck becomes bold.
Merrily sing cuckoo.
Cuckoo, cuckoo.
You sing well, cuckoo.
Never shall you cease now.

LATIN TEXT:

Observe, Christians, what an honor!
The heavenly farmer [i.e., Father], because of
    the blemish of the vine, not sparing His Son,
    exposed him to the destruction of death.
[He] Who delivers half-alive captives from
    punishment to life, and crowns [them] with
    himself in the heavenly throne.

—Latin translated by Fr. Dick John

PES:

Sing cuckoo now, Sing cuckoo.

Sing cuckoo, Sing cuckoo now.

Hildegard von Bingen (1098–1179)

PATRIARCHAE ET PROPHETAE
Qui sunt hi, qui ut nu-bes?

VIRTUTES
O an-ti-qui sancti, quid admirami-ni in no-bis? Ver — bum De — i cla-rescit in forma ho-mi-nis, et id-e-o fulge — mus cum il-lo, æ-di-fican-tes membra su-i pul-chri corpo — ris.

PATRIARCHAE ET PROPHETAE
nos sumus radi-ces et vos ra-mi, fructus vi-ven-tis o-culi, et nos um-bra in il-lo fu — i-mus.

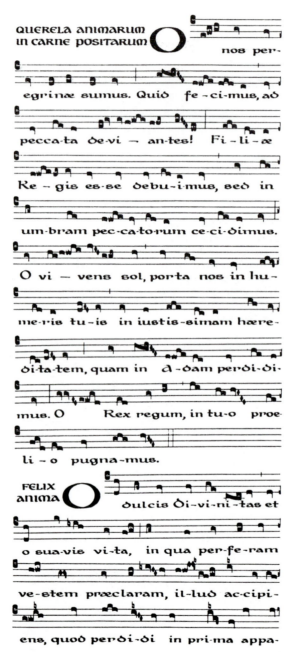

QUERELA ANIMARUM IN CARNE POSITARUM
O nos per-egrinæ sumus. Quid fe-ci-mus, ad peccata de-vi — an-tes! Fi — li — æ Re — gis es-se debu-i-mus, sed in um-bram pec-ca-to-rum ce-ci-dimus. O vi — vens sol, por-ta nos in hu-me-ris tu-is in iustis-simam hære-di-ta-tem, quam in A-dam perdi-di-mus. O Rex regum, in tu-o proe-li-o pugna-mus.

FELIX ANIMA
O dulcis Di-vi-ni-tas et o sua-vis vi-ta, in qua per-fe-ram ve-stem præclaram, il-lud ac-cipi-ens, quod perdi-di in pri-ma appa-

ri-ti-one, ad te sus-pi-ro et o-mnes vir-tu-tes in-vo-co.

VIRTUTES
O fe-lix a-ni-ma et o dulcis cre-atu — ra De-i, quæ æ-di-fi — ca-ta es in pro-fun-da al-titu-di-ne sa-pi-enti-æ De-i, mul — tum a-mas.

FELIX ANIMA
O li-benter ve-ni-am ad vos, ut præbe-a-tis mi-hi osculum cor-dis.

VIRTUTES
nos de-bemus mi-li-ta — re tecum, o fi-li-a Re-gis.

SED GRAVATA ANIMA CONQUERITUR
O gravis la-bor et o durum pondus, quod habe-

From Hildegard von Bingen: LIEDER, ed. Pudentiana Barth, M. Immaculata Ritscher, and Joseph Schmidt-Gorg (Salzburg, Austria: Otto Müller Verlag, 1969). Used by permission.

See DWM p. 92.

o in ve-ste huius vi-tæ, qui-a ni-mis gra-ve mi-hi est contra car-nem pu-gnare.

VIRTUTES AD ANIMAM ILLAM O a-ni-ma, volun-ta-te De-i consti-tu-ta, et o fe-lix in-strumentum, qua-re tam de-bi-lis es contra hoc, quod De-us contri-vit in virgi-ne-a natu-ra? Tu de-bes in no-bis su-pe-ra-re Di-a-bo-lum.

ANIMA ILLA Succur-ri-te mi-hi ad-iu-van-do, ut pos-sim sta-re.

SCIENTIA DEI AD ANIMAM ILLAM Vi-de quid il-lud sit, quo es indu-ta, fi-li-a salva-ti-o-nis, et e-sto sta-bi-lis et num-quam ca-des.

INFELIX ANIMA O nesci-o quid fa-ci-am aut u-bi fu-gi-am. O væ mi-hi, non pos-sum perfi-cere hoc, quo sum indu-ta. Cer-te il-lud vo-lo ab-i-ce-re.

VIRTUTES O infe-lix consci-en-ti-a, o mi-se-ra anima, qua-re abs-condis faci-em tu-am coram Cre-a-tore tu-o?

SCIENTIA DEI Tu ne-scis nec vi-des nec sa-pis il-lum qui te con-sti-tu-it.

ANIMA ILLA De-us cre-a-vit mun-dum, non faci-o il-li in-iu-ri-am,

sed vo-lo u-ti il-lo.

STREPITUS DIABOLI AD ANIMAM ILLAM: Fatue! fatue! quid prodest tibi labora-re? Respice mundum, et amplectetur te magno honore.

VIRTUTES O plan-gens vox est hæc maxi-mi do-lo-ris. Ach! ach! quædam mi-ra-bi-lis victo-ri-a in mi-ra-bi-li de-si-de-ri-o De-i sur-rexit, in qua de-lecta-ti-o car-nis se la-tenter abs-condit. He-u! he-u! u-bi vo-lun-tas crimina ne-sci-vit, et u-bi de-si-de-ri-um homi-nis la-sci-vi-am fu-git. Luge, lu-ge ergo in his, inno-cen-ti-a, quæ in pu-do-re bo-no in-te-gri-

ta - tem non a - mi - si-sti, et quæ a -

va-ri-ti-am guttu - ris an-ti-qui

serpen - tis i-bi non de - vo -

ra — sti.

DIABOLUS: Quæ est hæc potestas, quod nullus sit præter Deum? Ego autem dico: Qui voluerit me et voluntatem meam sequi, dabo illi omnia. Tu vero tuis sequacibus nihil habes, quod dare possis, quia etiam vos omnes nescitis quid sitis.

HUMILITAS E -go cum me-is so-da-

libus be-ne sci-o, quod tu es il-le

antiquus dra-co, qui su-per sum-

mum vo-la-re vo-lu-i-sti, sed i-pse

Deus in a-bys-sum pro-ie-cit te.

VIRTUTES n os autem omnes in

excel-sis ha-bi-ta-mus.

HUMILITAS E -go humi-li-tas, re-

gi-na virtu-tum, di-co: Ve-ni-te ad

me, virtu-tes, et enutri-am vos

ad requi-ren-dam perdi-tam drach-

mam et ad co-ro-nan-dum in per-se-

ve-ran-ti-a fe — li-cem.

VIRTUTES O glori-o-sa regi-na

et o sua-vis-si-ma me-di-atrix, li-

ben-ter ve-ni-mus.

HUMILITAS J de-o di-lec-tis-simæ fi-

li — æ, tene-o vos in rega-li

tha-la-mo.

CARITAS E -go ca-ri-tas, flos a-

ma-bi-lis, ve-ni-te ad me, vir-tu-tes,

et perdu-cam vos in can-di — dam

lucem flo-ris vir — gæ.

VIRTUTES O di-lectis-sime flos,

ardenti desideri-o cur-ri-mus

ad te.

TIMOR DEI E -go timor De-i, vos

felicissi-mas fili — as præ-pa-

ro, ut in-spi-ci-a-tis in De-um

vi — vum et non pere-a-tis.

VIRTUTES O timor, val-de u-ti-

lis es no-bis, ha-be-mus e-nim

per-fe-ctum stu-di — um numquam

a te se-pa-ra - ri.

PATRIARCHAE ET PROPHETAE:
Qui sunt hi, qui ut nubes?

PATRIARCHS AND PROPHETS:
Who are these, who [are] like clouds?

VIRTUTES:
O antiqui sancti, quid admiramini in nobis? Verbum Dei clarescit in forma hominis, et ideo fulgemus cum illo, aedificantes membra sui pulchri corporis.

VIRTUES:
O ancient holy ones, what makes you wonder at us? The Word of God becomes clear [is made understandable] in the form of a man, and therefore we shine brightly with him, edifying members of his glorious body.

PATRIARCHAE ET PROPHETAE:
Nos sumus radices et vos rami, fructus viventis oculi, et nos umbra in illo fuimus.

PATRIARCHS AND PROPHETS:
We are the roots and you the branches, fruit of the living bud [eye], and we were a shadow in him [i.e., a reflection of him].

QUERELA ANIMARUM IN CARNE POSITARUM:
O nos peregrinae sumus. Quid fecimus, ad peccata deviantes! Filiae Regis esse debuimus, sed in umbram peccatorum cecidimus. O vivens sol, porta nos in humeris tuis in iustissimam haereditatem, quam in Adam perdidimus. O Rex regum, in tuo proelio pugnamus.

COMPLAINT OF SOULS PLACED IN FLESH [= bodies]:
O we are pilgrims. What we have done, straying into sins! We ought to be daughters of the King, but we fall into the shadow of sins. O living Sun, carry us on your shoulders into the most equitable inheritance, which, through Adam, we lost. O King of kings, we are fighting in your battle.

FELIX ANIMA:
O dulcis Divinitas et o suavis vita, in qua, perferam vestem praeclaram, illud accipiens, quod perdidi in prima apparitione, ad te suspiro et omnes virtutes invoco.

FORTUNATE SOUL:
O sweet Divinity and O delightful life, in which I shall wear radiant clothing, receiving that, which I lost in [my] first appearance, to you I sigh and I invoke all virtues.

VIRTUTES:
O felix anima et o dulcis creatura Dei, quae aedificata es in profunda altitudine sapientiae Dei, multum amas.

VIRTUES:
O fortunate soul and O sweet creation of God, you who have been created in the profound height of God's wisdom, you love much [many things].

FELIX ANIMA:
O libenter veniam ad vos, ut praebeatis mihi osculum cordis.

FORTUNATE SOUL:
O gladly will I come to you, so that you can offer me the kiss of [your] heart.

VIRTUTES:
Nos debemus militare tecum, o filia Regis.

VIRTUES:
Our duty is to fight with you, O daughter of the King.

SED GRAVATA ANIMA CONQUERITUR:
O gravis labor et o durum pondus, quod habeo in veste huius vitae, quia nimis grave mihi est contra carnem pugnare.

BUT THE TROUBLED SOUL COMPLAINS:
O the arduous labor and O the heavy burden that I have in the clothing of this life, because it is so difficult for me to fight against the flesh.

VIRTUTES AD ANIMAM ILLAM:
O anima, voluntate Dei constituta, et o felix instrumentum, quare tam debilis es contra hoc, quod Deus contrivit in virginea natura? Tu debes in nobis superare Diabolum.

VIRTUES, TO THAT SOUL:
O soul, created by the will of God, and O fortunate instrument, why are you so troubled against that, which God wiped out in the virgin nature? You must, through us, overcome the Devil.

ANIMA ILLA:
Succurrite mihi adiuvando, ut possim stare.

THAT SOUL:
Hasten to aid me, so that I can stand firm.

SCIENTIA DEI AD ANIMAM ILLAM:
Vide quid illud sit, quo es induta, filia salvationis, et esto stabilis et numquam cades.

KNOWLEDGE OF GOD, TO THAT SOUL:
Consider what it is that you are clothed in, daughter of salvation, and be firm and you will never fail.

INFELIX ANIMA:
O nescio quid faciam aut ubi fugiam. O vae mihi, non possum perficere hoc, quo sum induta. Certe illud volo abicere.

UNHAPPY SOUL:
O, I know not what to do or where to flee. O, woe is me, I cannot wear to the end this [garment] in which I am clothed. Certainly, I wish I could cast this off.

VIRTUTES:
O infelix conscientia, o misera anima, quare abscondis faciem tuam coram Creatore tuo?

VIRTUES:
O unhappy conscience, O wretched soul, why do you hide your face in the presence of your Creator?

SCIENTIA DEI:
Tu nescis nec vides nec sapis illum qui te constituit.

KNOWLEDGE OF GOD:
You do not know, neither do you see nor understand the one who created you.

ANIMA ILLA:
Deus creavit mundum, non facio illi iniuriam, sed volo uti illo.

THAT SOUL:
God created the world, I do no harm to that one [Him], but I want to enjoy it [the world].

STREPITUS DIABOLI AD ANIMAM ILLAM:
Fatue! fatue! quid prodest tibi laborare? Respice mundum, et amplectetur te magno honore.

THE LOUD VOICE OF THE DEVIL, TO THAT SOUL:
Foolish! Idiotic! what do you gain by being distressed? Turn your attention to the world, and it will favor you with great honor.

VIRTUTES:
O plangens vox est haec maximi doloris. Ach! ach! quaedam mirabilis victoria in mirabili desiderio Dei surrexit, in qua delectatio carnis se latenter abscondit. Heu! heu! ubi voluntas crimina nescivit, et ubi desiderium hominis lasciviam fugit. Luge, luge ergo in his, innocentia, quae in pudore bono integritatem non amisisti, et quae avaritiam gutturis antiqui serpentis ibi non devorasti.

VIRTUES:
O this voice is bewailing of the greatest sorrow. Oh! oh! now a marvelous victory has arisen in the wonderful desire of God, in which delight of the flesh secretly concealed itself. Alas! alas! where the will knew no fault, and where man's desire fled from lust. Grieve, lament therefore in these [things], Innocence, who did not give up [your] integrity in [your] virtuous modesty, and who did not swallow the ancient serpent's gluttonous greed there.

DIABOLUS:
Quae est haec potestas, quod nullus sit praeter Deum? Ego autem dico: Qui voluerit me et voluntatem meam sequi, dabo illi omnia. Tu vero tuis sequacibus nihil habes, quod dare possis, quia etiam vos omnes nescitis quid sitis.

DEVIL:
What is this power, that no one can surpass God? But I say: Whoever is willing to follow me and my will, to that one I will give all things. Truly, you have nothing in your control, that you can give, because none of you know what you are.

HUMILITAS:

Ego cum meis sodalibus bene scio, quod tu es ille antiquus draco, qui super summum volare voluisti, sed ipse Deus in abyssum proiecit te.

VIRTUTES:

Nos autem omnes in excelsis habitamus.

HUMILITAS:

Ego humilitas, regina virtutum, dico: Venite ad me, virtutes, et enutriam vos ad requirendam perditam drachmam et ad coronandum in perseverantia felicem.

VIRTUTES:

O gloriosa regina et o suavissima mediatrix, libenter venimus.

HUMILITAS:

Ideo dilectissimae filiae, teneo vos in regali thalamo.

CARITAS:

Ego caritas, flos amabilis, venite ad me, virtutes, et perducam vos in candidam lucem floris virgae.

VIRTUTES:

O dilectissime flos, ardenti desiderio currimus ad te.

TIMOR DEI:

Ego timor Dei, vos felicissimas filias praeparo, ut inspiciatis in Deum vivum et non pereatis.

VIRTUTES:

O timor, valde utilis es nobis, habemus enim perfectum studium numquam a te separari.

—Hildegard von Bingen

HUMILITY:

I, with my companions, know well, that you are that ancient dragon, who wanted to fly above the highest, but God Himself threw you into the abyss.

VIRTUES:

However, we all dwell in the highest [i.e., heaven].

HUMILITY:

I, Humility, queen of the virtues, say: Come to me, Virtues, and I will nourish you to search for the lost drachma [i.e., coin] and to crown the fruitful [one] in persevering [i.e., the fruitful one who persists to the end].

VIRTUES:

O glorious queen and O most pleasant mediator, we come willingly.

HUMILITY:

For that, most beloved daughters, I keep you in the royal bed chamber.

CHARITY:

I am Charity, flower worthy to be loved, come to me, Virtues, and I will bring you into the white light of the flower of the branch [i.e., a genealogical branch].

VIRTUES:

O dearest flower, we run to you with burning desire.

FEAR OF GOD:

I, Fear of God, prepare you, most fortunate daughters, so that you may look upon the living God and not perish.

VIRTUES:

O Fear [of God], you are exceedingly useful to us; indeed, we have perfect devotion [zeal] never to be separated from you.

27 REIS GLORIOS, Chanson

Guiraut de Bornelh (c. 1140–c. 1200)

Reis glorios, verai lums e clartatz,
Deus poderos, senher, si a vos platz,
Al meu companh sias fizels aiuda,
Qu'eu non la vi pos la noitz ton venguda,
Et ades sera l'alba.

Glorious king, true light and clarity,
God Almighty, Lord, if it pleases Thee,
To my companion be a faithful aide,
For I have not seen him since night fell,
And soon it will be dawn.

See DWM p. 94.

28 KALENDA MAYA, Dansa

Raimbaut de Vaqueiras (d. 1207)

See DWM pp. 95, 102.

Kalenda maya
Ni fuelhs de faya
Ni chanz d'auzelh
Ni flors de glaya
Non es que'm playa,
Pros domna guaya,
Tro qu'un ysnelh
Messatgier aya
Del vostre belh
Cors, que'm retraya
Plazer novelh
Qu'Amors m'atraya,
E jaya E'mtraya
Vas vos, Domna veraya;
E chaya De playa
'Lgelos
Ans que'm n'estraya.

The First of May festival
Neither leaves of beech
Nor song of birds
Nor flower of lily [or, iris]
Are what please me,
Gracious, joyful lady,
Until I receive
A messenger
From your beautiful self,
That gives me
New pleasure,
Which Love brings me,
And joy, and I am drawn
To you, true lady;
And may he die of wounds,
The jealous one,
Before I am driven away.

29   PRENDÉS I GARDE, Rondeau

Guillaume d'Amiens (fl. late 13th century)

Prendés i garde, s'on mi regarde!
S'on mi regarde, dites le moi.
C'est tout la jus en cel boschaige:
Prendés i garde, s'on mi regarde!
La pastourele i gardoit vaches:
Plaisans brunette a vous m'otroi!
Prendés i garde, s'on mi regarde!
S'on mi regarde, dites le moi.

Take care that no one looks at me!
If anyone looks at me, tell me.
It is all down there in those woods.
Take care that no one looks at me!
The country girl tends the cows:
Pretty brunette, I am yours!
Take care that no one looks at me!
If anyone looks at me, tell me.

Transcribed from MS Reg. Christ. 1490, Biblioteca Vaticana, Rome.

See DWM p. 96.

30   DIEUS SOIT, Ballade with Refrain

Adam de la Halle, (c. 1245–c. 1288)

See DWM p. 96.

voir des ___ pai-re ___ sis   À no-hé-li ___ son.
mes de ___ ses nou-ris   Et si en-fan-çon.

Chorus

Dieus soit en ___ ches-te mai-son, ___ Et biens et joie à ___ fui-son!

31 A L'ENTRADA DEL TENS CLAR, Ballade

Anonymous

Solo
a
A l'en-tra-da del tens clar, E - y - a,   Chorus

Solo
Pir joi-e re-co-men-çar, E - y - a,   Chorus

Solo
a
E pir ja-lous ir-ri-tar, E - y - a,   Chorus

Solo
Vol la re-gi-ne mo-strar K'ele est si a-mo-

Chorus
b
rou-se.   A - la-vi', ___ a-la-vi - e,

Ja- ___ lous, ___ las-saz ___ nos, las-saz ___

nos bal-lar ___ en-tre ___ nos, ___ en-tre ___ nos.

Dieus soit en cheste maison,
Et biens et joie à fuison!

No sires Noueus
Nous envoie à ses amis,
Ch'est as amoureus
Et as courtois bien apris
Pour avoir des pairesis
À no hélison.

Nos sires est teus
Qu'il prieroit à envis,

Mais as frans honteus
Nous a en son lieu tramis
Qui sommes de ses nouris
Et si enfançon.

Dieus soit en cheste maison,
Et biens et joie à fuison!

—Adam de la Halle

God be in this house,
And well-being and joy abundantly!

Our sovereign lord
Sends us to his friends;
That is, to the enamoured
And to the polite, well-bred [persons],
To have some of paradise
Have mercy on us.

Our lord is such [a person]
That he would pray against the grain [i.e., even
when he did not feel like it];
But to the reluctant [or, disreputable] Franks
He sent us in his stead,
Who are [members] of his family
And as babies.

God be in this house,
And well-being and joy abundantly!

A l'entrada del tens clar, Eya,
Pir joie recomençar, Eya,
E pir jalous irritar, Eya,
Vol la regine mostrar
K'ele est si amorouse.
Alavi', alavie,
Jalous, lassaz nos,
lassaz nos ballar entre nos,
entre nos.

When the good weather comes, Eya,
to bring back joy, Eya,
and to annoy jealous ones, Eya,
I wish to show the queen
for she is so much in love.
On your way, on your way,
jealous ones, leave us,
leave us to dance among ourselves,
among ourselves.

Transcribed from MS Fr. 20050, fol. 82v.

See DWM p. 96.

32 OR LA TRUIX, Virelai

Anonymous

Or la truix trop aspre- te, Voir, voir! A ceu k'elle est simple- te. Trop pour ou tre cui- dies me tains Cant je cui-dole es-tre cer-tains De ceu loe n'a ve-rai des mois. Oix! Oix! C'est ceu ke plus me bles- ce. Or la truix trop as-pre- te, Voir, voir! A ceu k'elle est simple- te.

Or la truix trop asprete, Voir, voir!	I find her much too difficult, indeed!
A ceu k'elle est simplete.	Because she is so simple.
Trop pour outre cuidies me tains	Much too presumptuous did I act,
Cant je cuidole estre certains	Though I felt positively sure
De ceu loe n'a verai des mois. Oix! Oix!	Of what I shall not have for months, alas!
C'est ceu ke plus me blesce.	'Tis that which hurts me most of all.
Or la truix trop asprete, Voir, voir!	I find her much too difficult, indeed!
A ceu k'elle est simplete.	Because she is so simple.

Transcribed from MS Montpellier H196, fol. 338.

See DWM p. 96.

33 LE JEU DE ROBIN ET DE MARION, "Robins m'aime"
Rondeau

Adam de la Halle (c. 1245–c. 1288)

Ro-bins m'ai-me, Ro-bins m'a, Ro-bins m'a de-man-dé-e, si m'a-ra. Ro-bins m'a-ca-ta co-te-le D'es-car-la-te bone et be-le. Sous-ka-nie et chain-tu-rele, A leur i va! Ro-bins m'ai-me, Ro-bins m'a, Ro-bins m'a de-man-dé-e, si m'a-ra.

Robins m'aime, Robins m'a,	Robin loves me, Robin has me,
Robins m'a demandée, si m'ara.	Robin has asked me, if he will have me.
Robins m'acata cotele	Robin bought me a robe
D'escarlate bone et bele,	Of beautiful, superior quality cloth,*
Souskanie et chainturele,	A smock and a narrow girtle.
A leur i va.	For them I consent.**
Robins m'aime, Robins m'a,	Robin loves me, Robin has me,
Robins m'a demandée, si m'ara.	Robin has asked me, if he will have me.

— Adam de la Halle

Escarlate = cloth of superior quality, of various colors; *bone et bele* reenforce the fact that the cloth is good and lovely and of excellent quality.

**A leur i va = an idiomatic expression, ancient form of the modern *Va pour cela!* (literally, I go for that!) meaning I agree, or I consent.

See DWM p. 98.

34 A CHANTAR MES AL COR, Trobar

Beatritz, Countess of Dia (born c. 1140)

A chan-tar m'es al cor que non deu-ri- e. Tant mi ran-cun cele a qui sui a-migs. Et si l'am mais que

Source: Lyrics and music in MS fr. 844, fol. 204, Bibliothèque nationale, Paris.

See DWM p. 99.

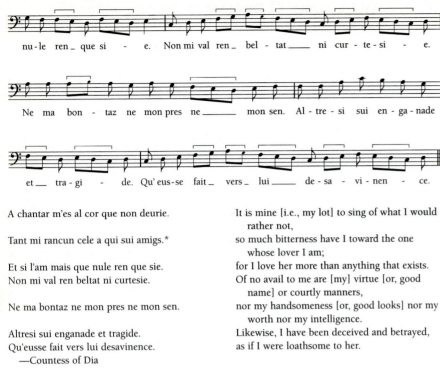

nu-le ren que si - e. Non mi val ren bel-tat ___ ni cur-te-si - e.

Ne ma bon-taz ne mon pres ne ___ mon sen. Al-tre-si sui en-ga-nade

et tra-gi - de. Qu'eus-se fait ___ vers ___ lui ___ de-sa-vi-nen - ce.

A chantar m'es al cor que non deurie.	It is mine [i.e., my lot] to sing of what I would rather not,
Tant mi rancun cele a qui sui amigs.*	so much bitterness have I toward the one whose lover I am;
Et si l'am mais que nule ren que sie.	for I love her more than anything that exists.
Non mi val ren beltat ni curtesie.	Of no avail to me are [my] virtue [or, good name] or courtly manners,
Ne ma bontaz ne mon pres ne mon sen.	nor my handsomeness [or, good looks] nor my worth nor my intelligence.
Altresi sui enganade et tragide.	Likewise, I have been deceived and betrayed,
Qu'eusse fait vers lui desavinence.	as if I were loathsome to her.
—Countess of Dia	

The lyrics usually recorded appear in another French manuscript, without music:

A chantar m'er de so qu'eu no volria	I must sing of that which I would rather not;
Tant me rancur de lui cui sui amia*	I am so aggrieved by him whose lover I am,
Car eu l'am mais que nulha ren que sia	for I love him more than anything that be.
Vas lui no.m val merces ni cortezia	Pity and courtliness do not help me with him,
Ni ma beltatz ni mos pretz ni mos sens,	Nor my beauty, nor my worth, nor my intelligence,
Qu'atressi.m sui enganad' e trahia	For also I am tricked and betrayed
Com degr' esser s'eu fos desavinens.	As I would deserve to be if I were loathsome.

*amigs = a male lover; amia = a female lover

35 CANTIGAS DE SANTA MARÍA
Anonymous

a PORQUE TROBAR, Prologo

Por - que tro - bar é cou - sa en que jaz

en - ten-di - men - to, por - en ___ quen o ___ faz

á - o d'a - ver, et de ra - zon as - saz, per - que en - ten - da et

sa - bia di - zer o que en - tend' et de di - zer lle

praz; ___ ca ___ ben tro - bar as - si s'á ___ de ffa - zer.

Este é o prologo das Cantigas de Santa Maria, ementando as cousas que á mester en o trobar.	This is the prologue to the Songs of Holy [or, Saint] Mary, listing the qualities that are important for writing verses [or, composing songs].
Porque trobar é cousa en que jaz entendimento, poren quen o faz áo d'aver, et de razon assaz, perque entenda et sabia dizer o que entend' e de dizer lle praz; ca ben trobar assi s'á de ffazer.	Because composing verse is an art that requires understanding, therefore, he who writes them must have it, and [also] sufficient judgment, to perceive and to know how to say what he understands and to express it in a pleasing manner; good verse is composed in this way.
E macar eu estas duas non ey	And though I do not have as much of the two [understanding and judgment]
com' eu querria, pero provarei a mostrar ende un pouco que sei, confiand' en Deus, ond' o saber ven,	as I wish I had, I will try to show the little that I know, trusting in God, from Whom all knowledge comes,
ca per ele tenno que poderei mostrar do que quero algua ren.	since through Him I think I may be able to show what I want to [express] in some way.

Transcribed from MS j.b.2 [MS b.I.2], El Escorial, (a) from fol. 1; (b) from fol. 29.

See DWM p. 99, and Fig. 7.4.

b   **DES OGE MAIS QUER EU TROBAR, Premeira cantiga de loor**

Des o - ge mais quer eu tro - bar pol-a Sen-nor_ on - rra -
da, en que Deus quis_ car - ne ___ fi - llar, bẽ - ey - ta et_ sa - gra -
da, por nos_ dar_ gran sol - da - da no seu rey - no_ et nos ___ er -
dar por_ seus de sa_ mas - na - da de vi - da per ___ lon - ga - da, sen
a - ver - mos pois_ a ___ pas - sar per mort' ou - tra_ ve - ga - da.

Des oge mais quer eu trobar
  pola Sennor onrrada,
en que Deus quis carne fillar
  bẽeyta et sagrada,
  por nos dar gran soldada
no seu reyno et nos erdar
  por seus de sa masnada
  de vida per longada,
sen avermos pois a passar
  per mort' outra vegada.

E poren quero começar
  como foy saudada
de Gabriel, u lle chamar
  fóy: "Ben aventurada
  Virgen, de Deus amada,
do que o mund' á de salvar
  ficas ora prennada;
  e demais ta cunnada*
Elisabeth, que foi dultar,
  é end' envergonnada . . ."

From today on I want to compose songs
  to that honored Lady,
in whom God chose to become flesh,
  blessed and holy,
  to give us the great reward
of His kingdom and to receive us
  as His own with the inheritance
  of eternal life,
without us having to pass through
  death once again.

And therefore I want to begin
  as you were greeted
by Gabriel, who announced
  to you: "Most favored
  Virgin, beloved of God,
you now become pregnant with Him
  who is to save the world;
  and, moreover, your cousin
Elisabeth, who once doubted,
  now is ashamed . . ."**

*literally, cunnada = sister-in-law; however,
  Elisabeth was Mary's cousin.

**Elisabeth is ashamed because she doubted the
  prophecy that she would become pregnant.

Additional verses relate to the other Six Joys: the Nativity, Epiphany, Resurrection, Ascension,
Pentecost, and Mary's coronation as Queen of Heaven.

---

36   **GLORIA 'N CIELO, Lauda**

Anonymous

[Ripresa]
Glo - ri - a in cie - lo_ e pa - ce ___ in ter - ra:

[Stanza]
nat' è'l no - stro_ sal - va - to - re. Nat' è Cri - sto_ glo - ri - o - so,
l'al - to Di - o ma - ra - vi - glio - so; fac - to è om de -
si - de - ro - so lo ___ be - ni - gno ___ Cre - a - to - re.

RIPRESA:*
Gloria 'n cielo e pace in terra:
nat' è'l nostro salvatore.

Nat' è Cristo glorioso,
l'alto Dio maraviglioso;
facto è om desideroso
lo benigno Creatore.

Della virgine sovrana
rilucente stella diana,
delli erranti tramontana,
puer nato della fiore.

Pace 'n terra sia cantata
gloria 'n ciel desiderata;
la donc̣ ella consecrata
parturit' à 'l salvatore.

REFRAIN:
Glory in heaven and peace on earth:
Born is our Savior.

Born is the glorious Christ,
the high marvelous God;
the benign Creator
has made a desirable man.

Of the sovereign virgin
a shining morning star,
of the wandering north wind,
a son born of the flower.

Sing peace on earth and
desire glory in heaven;
the consecrated maiden
has given birth to the Savior.

*Ripresa is sung at the beginning of the lauda and at the end of each stanza.

See DWM p. 100.

37 PALÄSTINALIED, Crusade Song

Walter von der Vogelweide (c. 1170–1228)

Nu al - rest leb' ich mir —— wer - de, —— sît mîn sun - dic ——
Lant daz hêre und — ouch die —— er - de, — dem man vil der —

ou - ge er - siht. —— Mir'st ge - schehn, des— ich ie— bat: ich bin —
ê - ren— giht. ——

ko - men —— an die — stat, da got men - nesch - lî - chen — trat.

Nu alrest leb' ich mir werde,
sît mîn sundic ouge ersiht.
Lant daz hêre und ouch die erde,
dem man vil der eren giht.

Mir'st geschehn, des ich ie bat:
ich bin komen an die stat,
da got menneschlîchen trat.

(There are 5 more 7-line stanzas.)

See DWM p. 101.

Now for the first time life has meaning for me,
since my sinful eyes beheld
the holy land and the very earth
that man honors so much [or, worships so much].

I have seen that for which I prayed:
I have come to the place
where God walked in human form.

38 KEYBOARD ESTAMPIE from ROBERTSBRIDGE CODEX

Anonymous

*No meter signature in MS. Dots mark off each breve. Bar lines are arbitrary in this transcription.

Transcribed from London, British Library Add. 28550, fol. 43v.

See DWM p. 103, and Fig. 7.6.

2. clos

Secundo punctus

Return to Primus punctus, and play it with repeats.
Then go to Tertius punctus.

Tertius punctus

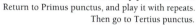

Return to Primus punctus, and play through only 1 time,
taking second ending. Then go to Quintus punctus.

Quintus punctus

Return to Primus punctus, and play it with repeats.
Then go to Quartus punctus.

Return to Primus punctus, and play it with repeats.
Then go to Sextus punctus

Quartus punctus

Sextus punctus

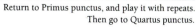

Return to Primus punctus, and play it with repeats; Fine.

*Probably scribal error; note should probably be f'.

39 GARRIT GALLUS—IN NOVA FERT—N[EUMA], Motet

Philippe de Vitry (1291–1361)

Source: MS fr. 146, fol. 44v, Bib. nat., Paris.

See DWM pp. 109, 110, and Plate 9.

TRIPLUM:

Garrit Gallus flendo dolorose,

Luge quippe Gallorum concio,

Que satrape traditur dolose,
Ex cubino sedens officio.
Atque vulpes, quamquam vispilio
In Belial vigens astucia,
De leonis consensu proprio
Monarchisat, atat angaria.
Rursus, ecce, Jacob familia
Pharaone altero fugatur;
Non ut olim Iude vestigia
Subintrare potens, lacrimatur.
In deserto fame flagellatur,
Adiutoris carens armatura,
Quamquam clamat, tantum spoliatus,
Continuo forsan moritura.
Miserorum exulum vox dura!
O Gallorum garritus doloris,
Cum leonis cecitas obscura

Fraudi paret vulpis proditoris.
Eius fastus sustinens erroris
Insurgito: alias labitur
Et labetur quod habes honoris,
Quod mox in facinis tardis ultoribus itur.

TRIPLUM:

The cock [or, Gaul = Frenchman] babbles,
    lamenting sorrowfully,
for, the assembly of cocks [or, Gauls = the
    French nation] mourns,
because it is deceived by the crafty satrap,
dutifully sitting in chambers.
And the fox,* like a nocturnal robber,
In Belial flourishing with astuteness,
with the consent of the lion** himself,
rules like a monarch. Ah! virtual slavery.
Behold, once again, Jacob's family
is put to flight by another pharaoh;
not, as formerly, vestiges being able
to escape into Judah, they weep.
In the desert they are stricken by famine.
Lacking the help of arms,
although they cry out, still they are robbed;
as a consequence, perhaps they will die.
O harsh voice of the wretched exiles!
O babbling of the mournful cocks [or, Gauls],
since the dark blindness [i.e., lack of discern-
    ment] of the lion
is subject to the wrongdoing of the traitor fox.
The arrogance of his misdeeds enduring,
rise up in revolt: or what you have
of honor is being and will be lost,
because, if avengers are slow, [people] will
    soon turn to villainy.

*Enguerran de Marigny, who was chief
    councillor to King Philip IV
**the King of France

DUPLUM:

In nova fert animus mutatus
Dicere formas.
Draco nequam quem olim penitus
mirabili crucis potencia
debellavit Michael inclitus,
Mox Absalon munitus gracia,
Mox Ulixis gaudens facundia,
Mox lupinis dentibus armatus,
Sub Tersitis miles milicia,
Rursus vivit in vulpem mutatus,
Cauda cuius, lumine privatus Leo,
Vulpe imperante, paret.
Oves suggit pullis saciatus.

Heu! suggere non cessat et aret.

Ad nupcias carnibus non caret.

Ve pullis mox, ve ceco leoni!

Coran Christo tandem ve draconi.

TENOR:

From the chant Neuma.

DUPLUM:

"My mind is set to tell of bodies changed into
    new forms." [Ovid: *Metamorphoses*, I, 1.]
The evil dragon that renowned Michael
once defeated by the power
of the marvelous cross,
Next Absalom endowed with grace,
Next Ulysses' delightful eloquence,
Next, armed with wolfish teeth,
a soldier in military service under Thersites,
Once more, he lives changed into a fox,
whose tail the Lion, deprived of sight,
obeys, the fox holding political power.
He [i.e., fox] sucks [the blood of] sheep and is
    satiated with young chickens.
Alas! he does not cease sucking and [still] he
    thirsts.
At wedding feasts he does not abstain from
    meats.
Now, woe to the young chickens, woe to the
    blind lion!
Finally, in the presence of Christ, woe to the
    dragon.

40 DETRACTOR EST—QUI SECUNTUR—VERBUM INIQUUM, Motet

Philippe de Vitry (1291–1361)

See DWM p. 110.

TRIPLUM:

Detractor est nequissima vulpis.
Per ses mesdis grieve autrui et lui pis,

Sed non minus adulator blandus,
Car il deçoit roys, princes, contes, dus.

Omnibus sunt tales fugiendi,
et li uns plus que li autres, s'en di.

TRIPLUM:

A disparager is the most worthless fox.
Through his slanders [he] harms others and
   himself worse,
But [he is] no less a bland flatterer,
Because he deceives kings, princes, counts,
   dukes.
Such [persons] are to be avoided by all,
and some more than others.

Much of the remainder of the text is garbled and meaningless, and some of it is corrupt. The main subject continues to be the evil caused by slander and disparagers.

DUPLUM:

Qui secuntur castra sunt miseri,
car pouvrement sont service meri
fidelibus qui bene serviunt
sanz mesprison et de vrai cueur seri:
de calice tales bibunt meri.

DUPLUM:

Those who follow camps are wretched,
because their services are poorly rewarded
by the faithful [persons] whom they serve well
without error and with true, kind heart[s]:
from the chalice such [persons] drink pure
   [wine].

From this point on the text is corrupt.

TENOR:

Verbum iniquum et dolosum abhominabitur
   Dominus.

TENOR:

An iniquitous and deceitful word will be an
   abomination to the Lord.

41 MESSE DE NOSTRE DAME, Agnus Dei

Guillaume de Machaut (1300–1377)

See DWM p. 114.

Agnus Dei, qui tollis peccata mundi,
  miserere nobis.
Agnus Dei, qui tollis peccata mundi,
  miserere nobis.
Agnus Dei, qui tollis peccata mundi,
  dona nobis pacem.

Lamb of God, who takest away the sins
  of the world, have mercy on us.
Lamb of God, who takest away the sins
  of the world, have mercy on us.
Lamb of God, who takest away the sins
  of the world, give us peace.

MA FIN EST MON COMMENCEMENT, Rondeau

Guillaume de Machaut (1300–1377)

See DWM p. 116.

Ma fin est mon commencement	My end is my beginning
Et mon commencement ma fin.	and my beginning my end.
Et teneure vraiement.	And holds indeed.
Ma fin est mon commencement.	My end is my beginning.
Mes tiers chans trois fois seulement	My third one time only
Se retrograde et einsi fin.	is retrograde and ends thus.
Ma fin est mon commencement	My end is my beginning
Et mon commencement ma fin.	and my beginning my end.

NON AL SUO AMANTE, Madrigal

Jacopo da Bologna (fl. 1340–1360)

See DWM p. 118.

a - mo - ro - so _____ ge - lo.

a - mo - ro - so _____ ge - lo.

1. Non al suo amante più Diana piaque,
   Quando per tal ventura tuta nuda
   La vide in mezzo de le gelide acque,

2. Ch'a me la pastorella alpestra e cruda

   Posta a bagnar un leggiadretto velo,
   Ch'a l'aura il vago e biondo capel chiuda,

RIPRESA:

Tal che mi fece, quando gli arde 'l celo,

Tuto tremar d'un amoroso gelo.

—Francesco Petrarch

1. Diana did not please her lover more
   When by chance he saw her completely
   nude
   In the midst of the icy waters,

2. Than [pleases] me the rustic and cruel
   shepherdess
   Intent on washing a gossamer veil,
   That protects [her] pretty blond hair from
   the breeze,

REFRAIN:

So that it makes me, now when the sky
burns,
Tremble all over with an amorous chill.

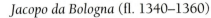

44   FENICE FU' E VISSI, Madrigal

Jacopo da Bologna (fl. 1340–1360)

Fe - ni - ce _____ fu' _ e

Fe - ni - ce _ fu'   e

vis-si _ pu-ra e mor - - - bi - da,   Et _

vis-si _ pu-ra e mor - - - bi - da, Et _ or _ son _ tras-mu-

or son _ tras-mu-ta-ta in u-na tor - - - to - ra   Che _

ta - ta in u - na   tor - - - - - to - ra

vo - lo   con   A - mor _____ per le _____ bel - l'or - -

Che vo-lo con A - mor   per _ le   bel - l'or - -

- - - - - - - to - ra.

- - - - - - to - ra.

See DWM p. 119.

45 TOSTO CHE L'ALBA, Caccia
Gherardello da Firenze (c. 1320–c. 1362)

Fenice fu' e vissi pura e morbida,
Et or son trasmutata in una tortora
Che vollo con Amor per le bell' ortora.

Arbor secho n' aqua torbida
No' me deleta, may per questo dubito,
Va nel' astate l'inverno ven e subito.

RIPRESA:

Tal vissi e tal me vivo e posso scrivere
Ch' a donna non è più chè onesta vivere.

 —Jacopo da Bologna

I was a phoenix and I lived pure and delicate,
And now I am transformed into a turtledove
That flies with Love through the beautiful
 orchards.

Dry trees and murky water
Do not delight me, but because of this doubt,
Go in summer, winter comes quickly.

REFRAIN:

So I lived and so I live and I can write
That for a woman there is no more than to live
 honestly.

See DWM p. 119

Tosto che l'alba del bel giorno appare

Isveglia li cacciator:
"Su, su, su, su, ch' egli è'l tempo!"
"Alletta li can, te, te, te, te,
Viola, te, Primera, te!"
Su alto al monte con buon cani al mano

E gli bracchetti al piano,
E ne la piaggia ad ordine ciascuno.
Io veggio sentir uno de' nostri miglior bracchi.

Starà avvisato.
"Bussate d'ogni lato ciascun
le macchie che Quaglina suona!"
"Ai-o, ai-o!" A te la cerbia viene.
Carbon la prese e in bocca la tene.

RITORNELLO:

Del monte que che v'era su gridava

al altra da l'altra e suo corno sonava.

As soon as the dawn of the beautiful day appears

the hunters arise:
"Up, up, get up! for it is time!
Call out the dogs, You, You [or, Here, here],
You, Viola! You, Primera!"
Up high on the mountain with good dogs at hand

and the hounds quiet,
and on the field everyone in order.
I see one of our best hounds scenting.

Stand alert!
"Let each one beat the bushes on all sides
for the quail calls!"
"Ayo, ayo!" The young doe is coming to you.
Carbon has seized her and holds her in [his] mouth.

RITORNELLO:

From the mountain that one who was there shouted

to one and to another and sounded his horn.

46 SÌ DOLCE NON SONÒ, Madrigal

Francesco Landini (1325–1397)

See DWM p. 119.

1. Sì dolce non sonò chol lir' Orpheo
   Quand' à se trasse fer' uciell' e boschi
   D'amor cantando d'infante di deo.

Orpheus with his lyre did not sound so sweet
When he drew toward himself wild beasts,
   birds, and woods,
Singing of love, of childhood, of God.

2. Come lo ghallo mio di fuor da boschi
   Con nota tale che gia ma' udita
   Non fu da Phylomena in verdi boschi.

As [did] my rooster from out of the woods
With such sound as never was heard
From Philomen in the green woods.

3. Ne più Phebo cantò quando schernita

   Da Marcia fu suo tibia in folti boschi
   Dove, vincendo, lo spoglio di vita.

No more did Phoebus play when his flute was
   scorned
By Marsyas in the thick woods
Where, victorious, he [i.e., Phoebus] deprived
   him [Marsyas] of life.

RITORNELLO:

   Di Theb' avanc' al chiudent' Anfione

   E fecto fa contrario del Gorgone.

RITORNELLO:

Amphion came to Thebes with the purpose of
   enclosing it
And acted in a manner contrary to that of the
   Gorgons.*

*Amphion's music caused the stones to move
to build the enclosing wall; the Gorgons
caused anyone who looked at them to turn to
stone.

47 NON AVRÀ MA' PIETÀ, Ballata

Francesco Landini (1325–1397)

See DWM p. 119.

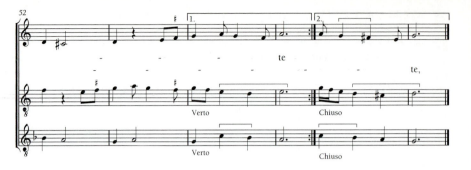

1. Non avrà ma' pietà questa mie donna,
   Se tu non faj, amore,
   Ch'ella sia certa del mio grande ardore.

2. S'ella sapesse quanta pena i' porto
   Per onestà celata nella mente

3. Sol per la sua bellecça, chè conforto
   D'altro non prende l'anima dolente,

4. Forse da lej sarebbono in me spente

   Le fiamme che la pare
   Di giorno in giorno acrescono'l dolore.

5. Non avrà ma' pietà questa mie donna,
   Se tu non faj, amore,
   Ch'ella sia certa del mio grande ardore.

   —B. d'Alessio Donati

This lady of mine will never have mercy,
if you do not see to it, love,
that she is certain of my great ardor.

If she was aware of how much pain I bear—
out of fairness, hidden in my mind—

only for her beauty, because nothing else
gives comfort to the mournful soul,

Perhaps by her there would be extinguished in
   me
the flame that seems
daily to increase pain in her.

This lady of mine will never have mercy,
if you do not see to it, love,
that she is certain of my great ardor.

48 SALVE, SANCTA PARENS, Carol

Anonymous

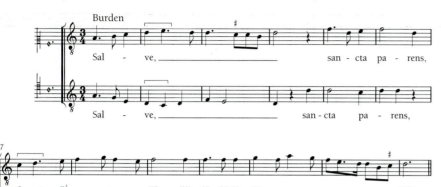

See DWM p. 122.

BURDEN:

Salve, sancta parens,
enixa puerpera regem.

VERSES:

Salve, porta paradisi,
felix atque fixa,
stella fulgens in sublimi
sidus enixa.

Salve, sancta dominatrix,
Virgo gloriosa,
Virgo imperatrix,
splendens velud rosa.

Salve, virgo benedicta,
mater orphanorum,
deprecamur ut delicta
tergas peccatorum.

BURDEN:

Hail, holy parent,
Mother who gave birth to a king.

VERSES:

Hail, gate of paradise,
blessed and secure,
star shining brightly on high
which gave birth to a constellation.

Hail, holy royal lady,
glorious Virgin,
Virgin empress,
resplendent as a rose.

Hail, blessed Virgin,
mother of orphans,
we beseech you to wipe away
the sins of transgressors.

49 QUAM PULCHRA ES, Motet

John Dunstable (c. 1390–1453)

See DWM p. 130.

Quam pulchra es et quam decora,
  carissima in deliciis.
Statura tua assimilata est palme,
  et ubera tua botris.
Caput tuum ut Carmelus,
  collum tuum sicut turis eburnea.
Veni, dilecte mi,
  egrediamur in agrum,
et videamus si flores fructus partuierunt,

  si floruerunt mala Punica.
Ibi dabo tibi ubera mea.
  Alleluia.

—Vulgate Bible, Canticum Canticorum IV

How beautiful you are and how graceful,
  dearest, for allurements.
Your stature is like unto a palm tree,
  and your breasts like the botrys.
Your head is like Carmel,
  your neck like an ivory tower.
Come, my beloved,
  let us go into the field,
and see whether the juice of the flower will
  bear fruit,
  whether the pomegranate trees bud.
There I will give you my loves.
  Alleluia.

50 VERGENE BELLA

Guillaume Du Fay (c. 1400–1474)

See DWM p. 132.

A. Vergene bella, che di sol vestita,
   Choronata di stelle al sommo sole
   Piacesti, sì, che'n te sua luce ascose;
   Amor mi spigne a dir di te parole:
   Ma non so'ncominzar senza tu aita,

   E di colui ch' amando in te si pose.

B. Invoco lei che ben sempre rispose
   Chi la chiamò con fede.
   Vergene, s' a mercede
   Miseria estrema dell' humane chose
   Già mai ti volse, al mio prego t' inchina.
   Soccorri alla mia guerra.

C. Bench' i' sia terra, e tu del ciel reina.

   —from Canzona CCCLXVI, Francesco Petrarch

Beautiful Virgin, who, clothed by the sun,
crowned with stars, so pleased the highest Sun
that he hid his light in you;
Love impels me to say [these] words to you:
But I cannot [I do not know how to] begin
   without your aid,
and [that] of that One who lovingly rested within you.

I invoke her who has always answered
whomever called her with faith.
Virgin, if extreme wretchedness
of human affairs ever moved you
to mercy, incline [your ear] to my prayer.
Uphold [or, help] me in my struggle.

Though I am earth [or, clay], and you [are]
   queen of heaven.

51   SE LA FACE AY PALE, Ballade

Guillaume Du Fay (c. 1400–1474)

See DWM p. 132.

Se la face ay pale,
La cause est amer.
C'est la principale,
Et tant m'est amer
Amer, qu'en la mer
Me voudroye voir;
Or, scet bien de voir,
La belle a qui suis,
Que nul bien avoir
Sans elle ne puis.

If the [i.e., my] face is pale,
the cause is love.
It is the principal [reason],
and it is so bitter for me
to love, that I would rather
see myself in the sea [i.e., drown];
Now, she can clearly see,
the beautiful [lady] whose I am,
that I cannot have any good [or, good thing]
without her.

Se ay pesante malle
De dueil a porter,
Ceste amour est male
Pour moy de porter;
Car soy deporter
Ne veult devouloir,
Fors qu'a son vouloir
Obeisse, et puis
Qu'elle a tel pooir,
Sans elle ne puis.

If I have a heavy burden
of grief to bear,
this love is hard
for me to endure;
Because she does not want
me to have any will
other than to obey
her will, and since
she has such power,
without her I cannot [help myself].

C'est la plus reale
Qu'on puist regarder,
De s'amour leiale
Ne me puis guarder,
Fol sui de agarder
Ne faire devoir
D'amours recevoir
Fors d'elle, je cuij;
Se ne veil douloir,
Sans elle ne puis.

She is the most royal [lady]
that one could consider [or, find].
I cannot keep myself
from loving her loyally.
I am mad to consider
not serving [her],
[and to consider] receiving love
elsewhere, I realize;
Although I do not want sorrow,
without her I am unable [to do anything].

52 NUPER ROSARUM FLORES—TERRIBILIS EST LOCUS ISTE, Motet

Guillaume Du Fay (c. 1400–1474)

Chant, LU, 1250, basis for motet Tenors:

See DWM p. 134, and Fig. 9.7.

Nuper rosarum flores
Ex dono pontificis
Hieme licet horrida
Tibi, virgo coelica,
Pie et sancte deditum
Grandis templum machinae
Condecorarunt perpetim.

May the roses recently [received]
as gift of the Pope
perpetually decorate,
even in harsh winter,
this grandly constructed temple
respectfully and solemnly dedicated
to you, heavenly Virgin.

Hodie vicarius
Jesu Christi et Petri
Successor EUGENIUS
Hoc idem amplissimum
Sacris templum manibus
Sanctisque liquoribus
Consecrare dignatus est.

Today, the vicar
of Jesus Christ, and the successor
to Peter, EUGENE,
has seen fit to consecrate
this most spacious temple
with his sacred hands
and with holy water.

Igitur, alma parens
Nati tui et filia,
Virgo decus virginum,
Tuus te FLORENTIAE
Devotus orat populus,
Ut qui mente et corpore
Mundo quicquam exorarit.

Therefore, gracious parent
and, at the same time, daughter of your son,
Virgin, glory of virgins,
your devoted people of FLORENCE
pray that those who entreat [or, pray]
with a pure mind and heart
may obtain whatever they pray for.

Oratione tua
Cruciatus et meritis
Tui secundum carnem
Nati domini sui
Grata beneficia
Veniamque reatum
Accipere mereatur.

O crucified One,
by your prayer and merits
may your children
born according to the flesh
be worthy to receive
gracious benefits and remission of sins
from the Lord.

Amen.

Amen.

TENOR:
Terribilis est locus iste

TENOR:
Awesome [or, terrible] is this place

74

MISSA L'HOMME ARMÉ, Agnus Dei

Guillaume Du Fay (c. 1400–1474)

See DWM p. 138.

*Canon: *Cancer eat plenus sed redeat medius.*

76

Agnus Dei, qui tollis peccata mundi,
  miserere nobis.
Agnus Dei, qui tollis peccata mundi,
  miserere nobis.
Agnus Dei, qui tollis peccata mundi,
  dona nobis pacem.

Lamb of God, who takes away the sins of the world,
  have mercy on us.
Lamb of God, who takes away the sins of the world,
  have mercy on us.
Lamb of God, who takes away the sins of the world,
  give us peace.

54   DE PLUS EN PLUS, Chanson

Binchois (Gilles de Binche; c. 1400–1460)

1. De plus en plus se renouvelle,
   Ma doulce dame gente et belle,
   Ma volonté de vous veir.

2. Ce me fait le tres grant desir
   Que j'ay de vous ouir nouvelle.

3. Ne cuidiés pas que je recelle,
   Comme a tous jours vous estes celle
   Que je vueil de tout obeir.

4. De plus en plus se renouvelle,
   Ma doulce dame gente et belle,
   Ma volonté de vous veir.

5. Helas, se vous m'estes cruelle,
   J'auroie au cuer angoisse telle
   Que je voudroie bien morir.

6. Mais ce seroit dans desservir,
   En soustenant vostre querelle.

7. De plus en plus se renouvelle,
   Ma doulce dame gente et belle,
   Ma volonté de vous veir.

8. Ce me fait le tres grant desir
   que j'ay de vous ouir nouvelle.

More and more is renewed,
my sweet lady, noble and beautiful,
my will to see you.

This gives me the very great desire
that I have to hear news of you.

Do not think that I hold back,
As always you are the one
whom I want to obey completely.

More and more is renewed,
my sweet lady, noble and beautiful,
my will to see you.

Alas, if you are cruel to me,
I shall have such anguish in my heart
that I would be willing to die.

But this would be without disservice [to you],
in upholding your cause.

More and more is renewed,
my sweet lady, noble and beautiful,
my will to see you.

This gives me the very great desire
that I have to hear news of you.

See DWM p. 142.

55 MISSA PROLATIONUM, Kyrie

Johannes Ockeghem (c. 1410–1497)

See DWM p. 155.

Kyrie eleison.
Christe eleison.
Kyrie eleison.

Lord, have mercy.
Christ, have mercy.
Lord, have mercy.

56   PARCE, DOMINE, Motet

Jacob Obrecht (c. 1450–1505)

Transcribed from Glareanus, *Dodekachordon* (published Basle, 1547), p. 260.

See DWM p. 160, and Fig. 10.6.

57 AVE MARIA, Motet

Josquin Desprez (c. 1440–1521)

Parce, Domine, populo tuo
quia pius es, et misericors.
Exaudi nos, in aeternum, Domine.

Have mercy, Lord, on your people,
for you are kind and merciful.
Hear us, for ever, Lord.

See DWM p. 164.

Ave Maria, gratia plena,
Dominus tecum, Virgo serena.

Ave cujus conceptio,
Solemni plena gaudio,
Coelestia, terrestria,
Nova replet laetitia.

Ave cujus nativitas
Nostra fuit solemnitas,
Ut lucifer lux oriens
Verum solem praeveniens.

Ave pia humilitas
Sine viro foecunditas
Cujus annunciatio
Nostra fuit salvatio.

Ave vera virginitas,
Immaculata castitas,
Cujus purificatio
Nostra fuit purgatio.

Ave praeclara omnibus
Angelicis virtutibus,
Cujus fuit assumptio
Nostra glorificatio.

O Mater Dei,
Memento mei.
Amen.

Hail, Mary, full of grace,
The Lord be with you, fair Virgin.

Hail [to you] whose conception,
full of solemn joy,
fills heavenly [and] earthly beings
with new gladness.

Hail [to you] whose nativity
was our solemn feast,
indeed [was] the morning star rising
preceding the true sun.

Hail, holy humility,
fruitful without man,
whose annunciation
was our salvation.

Hail, true virginity,
undefiled chastity,
whose purification
was our cleansing.

Hail [to you], admirable in all
angelic virtues,
whose assumption was
our glorification.

O, Mother of God,
remember me.
Amen.

58   ABSALON, FILI MI, Motet*

Josquin Desprez (c. 1440–1521)

Recorded a tritone higher.

See DWM p. 164.

Absalon, fili mi
fili mi, fili mi, Absalon.

Quis det
ut moriar pro te,
fili mi, Absalon?
Non vivam ultra,
sed descendam in infernum plorans.

Absalom, my son,
my son, my son, Absalom.

Who will grant
that I may die for you,
my son, Absalom?
Let me not live longer,
but let me descend into hell, weeping.

59 ZWISCHEN PERG UND TIEFFEM TAL, Lied

Heinrich Isaac (c. 1450–1517)

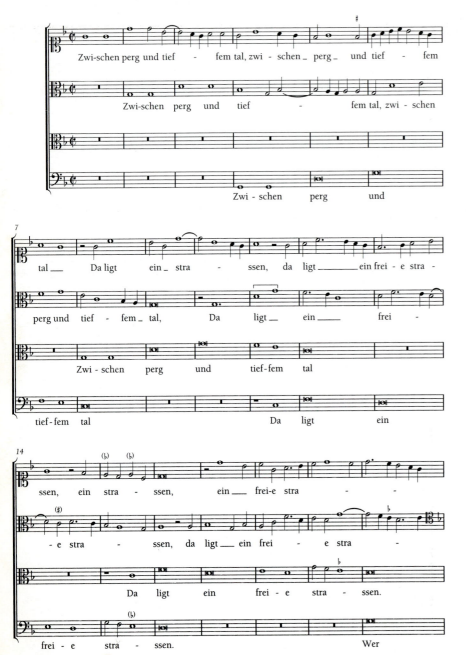

See DWM pp. 165, 189.

Zwischen perg und tieffem tal
Da ligt ein freie strassen.
Wer seinen püll nit haben mag,
Der müss yn faren lassen.

Far hin, far hin! Du hast die wal.
Ich kan mich dein wol massen.
Im jar sind noch vil langer tag,
Glück is in allen gassen.

Between the mountain and the deep valley
There lies a free highway.
Whoever does not wish to keep his love,
Must let him travel.

Travel there, travel there! You have the choice.
I can measure your welfare myself.
In a year the day will be much longer still,
Good fortune is in all paths.

60   SUPER FLUMINA BABYLONIS, Motet

Nicolas Gombert (c. 1495–c. 1560)

See DWM p. 167.

Super flumina Babylonis,
illic sedimus et flevimus
dum recordaremur tui, Sion.
In salicibus in medio ejus,
suspendimus organa nostra;
quia illic interrogaverunt nos,
qui captivos duxerunt nos,
verba cantionum;
et qui abduxerunt nos:
"Hymnum cantate nobis de canticis Sion."
Quomodo cantabimus canticum Domini
in terra aliena?

—Based on the Bible, Ps. 136:1–4

By the waters of Babylon,
there we sat down and wept
when we remembered you, Zion.
On the willows in the midst thereof,
we hung our instruments [harps];
for there they who have taken us
captive asked us,
the words of [our] songs;
and they who have abducted us [said]:
"Sing for us a hymn from the songs of Zion."
How shall we sing the Lord's song
in a strange land?

61 VICTIMAE PASCHALI LAUDES, Motet

Adrian Willaert (c. 1490–1562)

See DWM p. 169.

Victimae paschali laudes immolent Christiani.

Agnus redemit oves: Christus innocens Patri
    reconciliavit peccatores.
Mors et vita duello conflixere mirando: dux
    vitae mortuus, regnat vivus.

To the Paschal Victim let Christians offer
    songs of praise.
The Lamb has redeemed the sheep: sinless
    Christ has reconciled sinners to the Father.
Death and life have clashed in a miraculous
    combat: the leader of life died, [yet] living,
    he reigns.

62 EMENDEMUS IN MELIUS, Motet

Cristóbal de Morales (c. 1500–1553)

See DWM p. 170.

Emendemus in melius, quae ignoranter peccavimus: ne subito praeocupati die mortis,
quaeramus spatium paenitentiae, et invenire
non possimus.

Attende, Domine, et miserere: quia peccavimus
tibi.

ALTO II:

Memento homo, quia pulvis es, et in pulverem
reverteris.

—Alto II adapted from the Bible, Genesis 3:19

Let us make amends because, in ignorance, we
have sinned: not anticipating, suddenly, on
the day of death, we may seek a place of
repentance, and not be able to find [one].

Here [us], Lord, and have mercy: because we
have sinned against You.

ALTO II:

Remember, man, that you are dust, and to dust
you shall return.

63 OIMÈ EL CUOR, Frottola

Marco Cara (c. 1470–c. 1525)

See DWM p. 175.

Oimè el cuor, oimè la testa!
Chi non ama non intenda.

Oimè Dio, che error fece io!
Chi non falla non s'amenda.

Oimè Dio, che'l pentir mio!
Ad amar un cor fallace.

Dopo il fallo el pentir resta,
non mi da per questo pace.

Oimè el cuor, oimè la testa!
Oimè, el foco aspro e vivace,
mi consuma el tristo core.

Chi non ama non intenda,
Oimè Dio che'l fatto errore,
l'alma afflicta, mi molesta.

Alas, my heart; alas, my head!
Whoever does not love does not understand.

Alas, God, what a mistake I made!
Whoever does not sin needs not repent.

Alas, God, how I regret it!
Having catered [or, given in] to a sinful heart.

After sinning, it remains to repent,
for this reason I am given no peace.

Alas, my heart; alas, my head.
Alas, the fire, harsh and quick,
consumes my sad heart.

Whoever does not love does not understand,
Alas, God, what a mistake I have made,
my aggrieved spirit disturbs me.

64 QUANDO RITROVO LA MIA PASTORELLA, Madrigal

Costanzo Festa (c. 1480–1545)

See DWM p. 176.

Quando ritrovo la mia pastorella
Al prato con le pecor' in pastura,
Io mi gli accost' e presto la saluto.
La mi risponde, "Tu sia el benvenuto."
E poi gli dic' in quella,
"O gentil pastorella,
Non men crudel che bella,
Sei del mio ben ribella;
Deh non esser ver me cotanto dura."
Cosi rispond' anch' ella,
"Disposta son a quel tuo cordesia,
Ma se non hai denari, va alla tua via."

When I find my shepherdess
In the meadow, with the sheep in the pasture,
I approach her and quickly I greet her.
She answers me, "You are welcome."
And then I say to her,
"O gentle shepherdess,
No less cruel than beautiful,
You fight against my happiness.
Alas! Do not be so harsh to me."
She answers me thus,
"I am [well] disposed to your suit,
But if you do not have money, go on your way."

65 DA LE BELLE CONTRADE D'ORIENTE, Madrigal

Ciprano de Rore (1516–1565)

See DWM p. 177.

Da le belle contrade d'oriente
Chiara e lieta s'ergea Ciprigna, et io
Fruiva in braccio al divin idol mio
Quel piacer che non cape humana mente,

Quando sentii dopo un sospir ardente:
Speranza del mio cor, dolce desio,
Te'n vai, haime, sola mi lasci, adio.

Che sarà qui di me scura e dolente?
Ahi, crudo Amor, ben son dubiose e corte
Le tue dolcezze, poich' ancor ti godi
Che l'estremo piacer finisca in pianto.
Nè potendo dir più, cinseme forte,
Iterando gl' amplessi in tanti nodi,

Che giamai ne fer più l'edra o l'acanto.

From the fair regions of the east
Dawn rose, clear and glad, and I,
In the arms of my divine idol, was enjoying
That pleasure which no human mind can com-
   prehend,
When I heard, after an ardent sigh:
"Hope of my heart, sweet desìre,
You are going, alas! You are leaving me alone.
   Farewell!
What will become of me, gloomy and sad?
Ah, cruel Love! Uncertain and short are
Your sweetnesses, for you even rejoice
That the utmost pleasure should end in tears."
Unable to say more, she held me fast,
Repeating the embraces in so many entwin-
   ings,*
That never either ivy or acanthus made more.

*Literally, in so many knots

SOLO E PENSOSO, Madrigal

Luca Marenzio (c. 1553–1599)

See DWM p. 179.

et io con lu—i, et io con lu—i, et io con lu—i.

i, Cer-car non sò et io con lu—i.

me—co, et io con lu—i, et io con lu—i.

et io con lu—i, [et io con lu—i,] et io con lu—i.

car non sò] et io con lu—i, et io con lu—i.

Solo e pensoso i più deserti campi

Vò' misurando a passi tardi e lenti,
E gl' occhi porto per fuggir intenti

Dove vestiggio human l'arena stampi.

Altro schermo non trovo che mi scampi
Dal manifesto accorger de le genti;
Perchè negli atti d'allegrezza spenti
Di fuor si legge com' io dentro avampi.

Sì ch' io mi cred' homai che monti e piagge
E fiumi e selve sappian di che tempre
Sia la mia vita, ch' è celata altrui.

Ma pur sì aspre vie ne sì selvagge
Cercar non sò ch' Amor non venga sempre
Ragionando con meco, et io con lui.

—Petrarch

Alone and thoughtful, with lagging and slow
    steps
I pace the most deserted fields,
and I keep my eyes watchful in order to take
    flight
whenever human traces mark the earth.

I do not find any other shield that protects me
from the knowing looks of the people;
Because by my actions, drained of joy,
one reads from outside how I burn inside.

So that I now believe that mountains and shore
and rivers and forests know of what temper
my life is, that is hidden from others.

But yet I do not know how to seek pathways
so harsh or so wild that Love does not always
come for the purpose of reasoning with me,
    and I with him.

67 MORO, LASSO, AL MIO DUOLO, Madrigal
Carlo Gesualdo (c. 1561–1613)

E chi mi può dar vi—

Mo—ro, las—so, al _ mio duo—lo E chi mi può dar

Mo—ro, las—so, al mio duo—lo

Mo—ro, las—so, al mio duo—lo

Mo—ro, las—so, al mio duo—lo

—ta, E chi mi può dar vi—ta,

vi—ta, E chi mi può _ dar vi—

E chi mi può dar vi—ta, E chi mi può dar

E chi mi può dar vi—ta, E _ chi mi può

E chi mi può dar vi—

See DWM p. 179.

109

Moro, lasso, al mio duolo
E chi mi può dar vita,
Ahi, che m'ancide e non vuol darmi aita!

O dolorosa sorte,
Chi dar vita mi può, ahi, mi dà morte!

I am dying, wretched, in my grief,
And [the one] who is able to give me life,
Alas, is killing me and is not willing to give me
    aid!

O painful fate,
[The one] who is able to give me life, alas,
    gives me death!

68 SING WE AND CHANT IT, Ballett

Thomas Morley (c. 1557–1602)

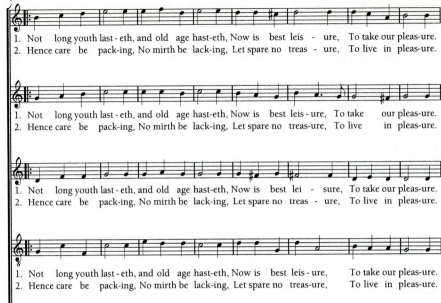

The words of the second stanza are not sung until the *entire* ballett, with repeats, has been sung to the words of the first stanza.

See DWM p. 180.

69 NON È SÌ DENSO VELO, Madrigal

Giaches de Wert (1535–1596)

See DWM p. 182.

Non è sì denso velo,
Se fosser monti sopra mont' imposti,
Nè sì remoto cielo,
Che possa far nascosti
E lontan quei bei lumi,
Che nè mari nè fiumi,
Nè paese longinqui,
Faran giamai che non mi sian propinqui.
I' gl' ho s'affissi a gl' occhi,
Ch' ogni sguardo ch' io scocchi
Parmi che quel splendor mi senda il viso
Ch' in vita mi mantien, poichè m' ha ucciso.

There is no veil so dense,
not even mountains piled on mountains,
nor is heaven so remote and far away,
that it could hide
those beautiful eyes [from me],
which neither seas nor rivers,
nor distant lands,
will ever cause not to be near to me.
I have stared into them so intensely
that it seems to me that wherever I look
their splendor comes into my face,
which keeps me alive, after having slain me.

70   À CE JOLY MOYS DE MAY, Chanson

Clément Janequin (c. 1485–1558)

À ce jo-ly moys, jo-ly moys, jo-ly moys de may, ce jo-ly, jo-ly

À ce jo-ly moys, ce jo-ly moys de may, jo - ly,

À ce jo-ly moys de may, ce jo - ly, jo-ly,

À ce jo - ly, ce jo - ly moys, ce

moys de may Fai-sons, fai - sons tous bon-ne che-re, fai-sons tous

jo - ly moys de may Fai - sons ___ tous bon-ne che -

jo-ly moys, ce jo-ly, jo-ly moys, ce jo-ly moys de may ___ Fai - sons ___

jo - ly moys de may Fai-sons, fai - sons tous bon-ne

bon - ne che - re. 1. Res-veil-lons nous, ne dor-mons plus Dan-sons, bal-lons, bal-
                   2. À bien pous-ser n'ay-ons vains cueurs Don-nons de-dans, de-

                   1. Res - veil - lons nous, ne dor-mons plus
                   2. À bien pous-ser n'ay - ons vains cueurs

_ tous bon-ne che - re. 1. Res-veil-lons nous, ne dor-mons plus Dan -
                        2. À bien pous-ser n'ay - ons vains cueurs Don -

che - re. 1. Res-veil-lons nous, ne dor-mons plus Dan - sons, bal-
           2. À bien pous-ser n'ay-ons vains cueurs Don - nons de-

See DWM p. 184.

lons, dan-sons, dan-sons, bal-lons et au sur - plus, Chas-cun fas - se
dans don-nons, don-nons de-dans, soy-ons vain - cueurs, Ce - luy de nous

Dan - sons, bal-lons, dan-sons, bal-lons et au sur - plus, Chas-cun fas - se
Don - nons de-dans, don-nons de-dans, soy-ons vain-cueurs, Ce - luy de nous

sons, bal-lons, bal-lons, dan-sons, dan-sons, bal-lons et au sur-plus ___ Chas - cun
nons de-dans, de-dans, don-nons, don-nons de-dans, soy-ons vain-cueurs, ___ Ce - luy

lons, bal-lons, dan-sons, dan-sons bal-lons et au sur-plus, Chas-cun fas - se
dans de-dans, don-nons, don-nons de-dans, soy-ons vain-cueurs, Ce - luy de nous

son es - say Pour se - re la crou-pie-re, la crou-pie - re, pour ser - re
le plus gay Si por - te la ban-nie-re, la ban-nie - re, si por - te

son es - say Pour ser-re la crou-pie - re, la crou-pie - re, pour ser - re
le plus gay Si por - te la ban-nie - re, la ban-nie - re, si por - te

fas - se son es - say Pour ser - re, pour ser - re la crou-pie - re, pour ser - re
de nous le plus gay Si por - te, si por - te la ban-nie - re, si por - te

son es - say Pour ser - re la crou-pie - re, la crou-pie - re, pour ser - re
le plus gay Si por - te la ban-nie - re, la ban-nie - re, si por - te

la crou - pie - re. À ce jo - ly, jo - ly moys,
la ban - nie - re.

la crou-pie - re. À ce jo - ly moys, à ce jo - ly
la ban - nie - re.

la crou-pie - re. À ce jo - ly moys, à ce
la ban - nie - re.

la crou-pie - re. À ce jo - ly, jo - ly moys de may
la ban - nie - re.

Dal Segno

REFRAIN:

À ce joly moys, ce joly moys de may
Faisons tous bonne chere.

1. Resveillons nous, ne dormons plus
Dansons, ballons et au surplus,

Chascun fasse son essay
Pour serre la croupiere.

REFRAIN:

À ce joly moys, *etc.*

2. À bien pousser n'ayons vains cueurs

Donnons dedans, soyons vainceurs,
Celuy de nous le plus gay
Si porte la banniere.

REFRAIN:

À ce joly moys, *etc.*

REFRAIN:

In this pretty month, this pretty month of May
Let us live very well!

Let us wake up, let us sleep no longer,
Let us dance, let us dance [or, have a ball],
     and, besides,
Let each one make his attempt
to tighten the crupper.

REFRAIN:

In this pretty month, *etc.*

To really incite [or, push], let us not have vain
     hearts.
Let us look within, let us be conquerors,
That one of us [who is] the liveliest
indeed, carries the banner [or, flag].

REFRAIN:

In this pretty month, *etc.*

71 Excerpt from REVECY VENIR DU PRINTEMPS, Musique mesurée

Claude Le Jeune (c. 1530–1600)

See DWM p. 186.

116

Repeat Rechant à 5

Repeat Rechant à 5.

RÉCHANT à 5:

Revoicy venir du printemps
L'amoureus le dous et beau temps.

CHANT à 2:

Le superbe cours du torrent
A repris le lit de ses bors,
De la mer le flot tougrondant
Ja toucalme et coy ne sort hors.
Le canard s'ebat à plonger,
Et folastre amour va cherchant,
Ja la grue a fait alonger
sa bataille à pointe fourchant.

RÉCHANT à 5:

Revoicy venir *etc.*

CHANT à 3:

Le soleil plu' beau se fait voir
Plu' serain, plu' clair, plu' vermeil,
Le nuage épais se voit choir
Dissipé du ray du grand oeil.
Mile bois de verd se font pleins,
Mile champs de verd se sont peins,
Mile prés de fleurs bigarrés.

RÉCHANT à 5:

Revoicy venir *etc.*

The original old French text, as printed in 1603, is:

REFRAIN:

Revecy venir du Printans
L'amoureuz' et belle saizon.

Le courant des eaus recherchant
Le canal d'été s'éclaircit:
Et la mer calme de ces flots
Amolit le triste courrous:

Le canard s'egaye plonjant,
Et se lave coint dedans l'eau:
Et la gru' qui fourche son vol
Retraverse l'air et s'en va.

REFRAIN, for 5 voices:

Here comes spring again
the lovely, sweet, and beautiful season.

VERSE, for 2 voices:

The superb course of the torrent [i.e., river]
has again filled its bed;
The all-raging mass of the sea
is now tranquil and does not flood.
The duck frolics to dive,
and goes seeking playful love.
Now the crane has stretched out
its neck, and is turning.

REFRAIN, for 5 voices:

Here comes *etc.*

VERSE, for 3 voices:

The sun appears more beautiful,
more serene, clearer, rosier;
The thick cloud disappears,
dissipated by the ray(s) of the great eye [i.e., sun].
A thousand woods are full of greenery;
a thousand fields are full of greenery;
a thousand meadows [are full of] variegated
    flowers.

REFRAIN, for 5 voices:

Here comes *etc.*

REFRAIN: Revecy *etc.*

Le Soleil éclaire luizant
D'une plus séreine clairté:
Du nuage l'ombre s'enfuit,
Qui se jou' et court et noircit
Et foretz et champs et couteaus.
Le labeur humain reverdit,
Et la pré découvre ses fleurs.

REFRAIN: Revecy *etc.*

72 APRIL IS IN MY MISTRESS' FACE, Madrigal

Thomas Morley (c. 1557–1602)

See DWM p. 187.

73 IN DARKNESS LET ME DWELL, Ayre

John Dowland (1563–1626)

See DWM p. 188.

74a MEIN G'MÜTH IST MIR VERWIRRET, Lied

Hans Leo Hassler (1562–1612)

See DWM pp. 189, 195.

Mein gmüth ist mir verwirret
Das macht ein Jungfrau zart
Bin gantz und gar verirret
Mein Hertz das krenckt sich hart
Hab tag und nacht kein ruh
Für allzeit grosse klag
Thu stets seufftzen und weinen
In trauren schier verzag.

My peace of mind is disturbed
This a tender maiden has caused
I am completely and entirely astray
My heart hurts badly
Day and night I have no rest
Always [there is] great complaint
Continual sighing and weeping
In utter sorrow despairing.

Ach dass sie mich thet fragen
Was doch dir ursach sey,
Warumb ich führ solch klagen,
Ich wolt irs sagen frey
Dass sie allein die ist
Die mich so sehr verwundt.
Köndt ich ir Hertz erweichen
Würd ich bald wider gesund.

Ah, if she were to ask me
What the matter is,
Why I am complaining so,
I would say to her freely
That she alone is the one
Who has wounded me so greatly.
If I could soften her heart
I would soon be healthy again.

Reichlich ist sie gezieret
Mit schön thugend ohn ziel
Höflich wie sie gebüret
Ihrs gleichen ist nich viel.
Für andern Jungkfraun zart
Führt sie allzeit den preiss.
Wann ichs anschau, vermeine
Ich sey im Paradeiss.

She is richly adorned
With beautiful virtue without end
As nobly as she is born
Not many are equal to her.
Against other tender maidens
She always wins the prize.
When I look at her, I think
I am in Paradise.

Ich kan nicht gnug erzehlen
Ihr schön und thugend vil
Für alln wolt ichs erwehlen
Wer es nur auch ir will
Dass sie ir Hertz und Lieb
Gegn mir wendet allzeit.
So würd mein schmertz und klagen
Verkehrt in grosse freud.

I cannot extol enough
Her beautiful and virtuous power
For the only thing I would choose
If it were her desire also
That she would turn her heart and love
Toward me forever.
Then would my pain and complaining
Change to great joy.

Aber ich muss auffgeben
Und allzeit traurig sein
Solts mir gleich kosten sLeben
Das ist mein gröste pein.
Dann ich bin ir zu schlecht
Darumb sie mein nicht acht.
Gott wolts für leid bewahren
Durch sein Göttliche macht.

But I must give up
And be sorrowful forever
Even if it should cost me my life.
That is my greatest pain.
Because I am too low for her,
That is why she does not consider me.
God will preserve me in [my] sorrow
Through His divine power.

74b O HAUPT VOLL BLUT UND WUNDEN, Chorale

J.S. Bach (1685–1750)

See DWM pp. 195, 314.

O Haupt voll Blut und Wunden,
voll Schmerz und voller Hohn!
O Haupt, zu Spott gebunden
mit einer Dornenkron!
O Haupt, sonst schön gezieret
mit höchster Ehr' und Zier,
jetzt aber hoch schimpfieret:
gegrüsset seist du mir!

Du edles Angesichte,
vor dem sonst schrickt und scheut
das grosse Weltgerichte,
wie bist du so bespeit!
Wie bist du so erbleichet,
wer hat dein Augenlicht,
dem sonst kein Licht nicht gleichet,
so schändlich zugericht'?

O head full of blood and wounds,
full of sorrow and full of scoffing!
O head, for mockery, wreathed
with a crown of thorns!
O head, once handsomely adorned
with highest honor and esteem,
but now highly insulted:
Let me hail You!

You, noble countenance,
before which the great Last Judgment
terrifies and cowers,
how You are spat upon!
How very pale you are!
Who has so shamefully treated
Your eyes' light [literally, eyesight]
which no other light equals?

75 TODOS LOS BIENES DEL MUNDO, Villancico

Juan del Encina (1468–c. 1530)

*All instruments but Arpa and Tamb^lo. play three measures as introduction.
See DWM p. 190.

123

R. Todos los bienes del mundo passan presto y su memoria, salvo la fama y la gloria.	All the goods [property] in the world and their memory pass quickly, except fame [reputation] and glory.
1. El tiempo lleva los unos a otros fortuna y suerte, y al cabo viene la muerte, que no nos dexa ninguno.	Time carries away some, others [are taken away] by fortune and luck, and in the end death comes, which leaves us with none.
R. Todos son bienes fortunos y de muy poca memoria, salvo la fama y la gloria.	All goods are from fortune and [are] of very short memory, except fame [reputation] and glory.
2. La fama vive segura, aunque se muera su dueño; los otros bienes son sueño y una cierta sepultura.	Fame [reputation] survives safely even if its owner dies; the other goods are a dream and [have] a certain grave.
R. La mejor y mas ventura passa presto y su memoria, salvo la fama y la gloria.	The best and greatest venture and its memory pass quickly, except fame [reputation] and glory.
3. Procuremos bona fama, que jamás nunca se pierde, árbol que siempre está verde y con el fruto en la rama.	Let us acquire good reputation, which never, never is lost, a tree that always is green and with fruit on the [its] branches.
R. Todo bien que bien se llama passa presto y su memoria, salvo la fama y la gloria.	All property that can be called good and its memory passes quickly, except fame [reputation] and glory.
—Juan del Encina	—Miguel Roig-Francolí

76   EGO SUM PANIS VIVUS, Motet

William Byrd (c. 1543–1623)

© 1998 by A-R Editions, Inc. Used with permission.

See DWM p. 201.

Ego sum panis vivus,
qui de coelo descendi.
Si quis manducaverit ex hoc pane,
vivet in aeternum.
Alleluia.

I am the living bread,
which came down from heaven.
If any man eats of this bread,
he shall live for ever.
Alleluia.

—Bible, John 6:51–52

77 LAUDA SION, Motet

Giovanni Pierluigi da Palestrina (c. 1525–1594)

See DWM p. 205.

Lauda Sion salvatorem,
lauda ducem et pastorem
in hymnis et canticis;
quantum potes, tantum aude,
quia major omni laude,
nec laudare sufficis.

Bone pastor, panis vere,
Jesu, nostri miserere;
tu nos pasce, nos tuere,
tu nos bona fac videre
in terra viventium.

Amen.

Zion, praise [your] Savior,
praise [your] leader and shepherd
in hymns and canticles;
as much as you are able, so much dare,
because [He is] greater than all praise,
nor can you praise [Him] enough.

Good shepherd, true bread,
Jesus, have mercy on us;
You feed us, protect us,
You make us see good things
in the land of the living.

Amen.

78 MISSA LAUDA SION, Kyrie

Giovanni Pierluigi da Palestrina (c. 1525–1594)

Kyrie eleison.
Christe eleison.
Kyrie eleison.

Lord have mercy.
Christ have mercy.
Lord have mercy.

See DWM p. 206.

79 O VOS OMNES, Motet

Tomás Luis de Victoria (1548–1611)

See DWM p. 207.

O vos omnes, qui transitis per viam,
attendite universi populi et videte dolorem meum
si est dolor similis sicut dolor meus.

O, all you who pass along the way,
behold, all people, and see my sorrow,
if there is any sorrow like unto my sorrow.

—Adapted from the Bible, Lamentations 1:12

80 TRISTIS EST ANIMA MEA, Motet

Orlande de Lassus (1532–1594)

See DWM p. 209.

e - go va - dam im - mo-la - ri pro _____ vo - bis.

- go va - dam im - mo-la - ri] _____ pro vo - bis.

e - go va - dam im - mo-la - ri _____ pro _____ vo - bis.

e - go va - dam im - mo-la - ri pro _____ vo - bis.

e - go va - dam im - mo-la - ri pro vo - bis.

Tristis est anima mea usque ad mortem;
sustinete hic, et vigilate mecum:
nunc videbitis turbam, quae circumdabit
  me:
vos fugam capietis, et ego vadam immolari
  pro vobis.

My soul is sorrowful even unto death;
tarry here, and watch with me:
now you will see the crowd that will surround
  me:
you will take flight, and I shall go to be
  sacrificed for you.

—from the Bible, Matt. 26:38, Mark 14:34, and Liber Usualis, 635

81 SONATA PIAN' E FORTE

Giovanni Gabrieli (c. 1553–1612)

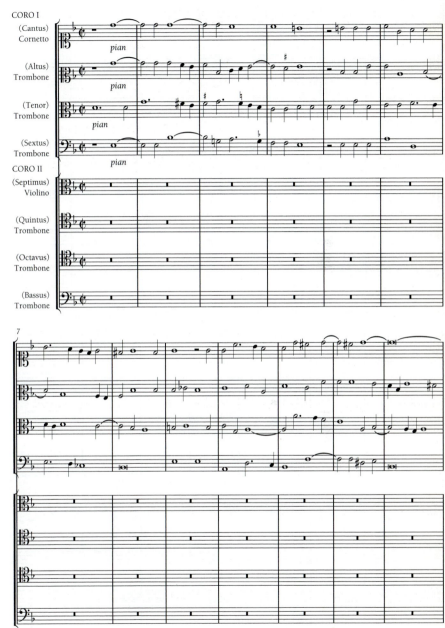

See DWM pp. 212, 225.

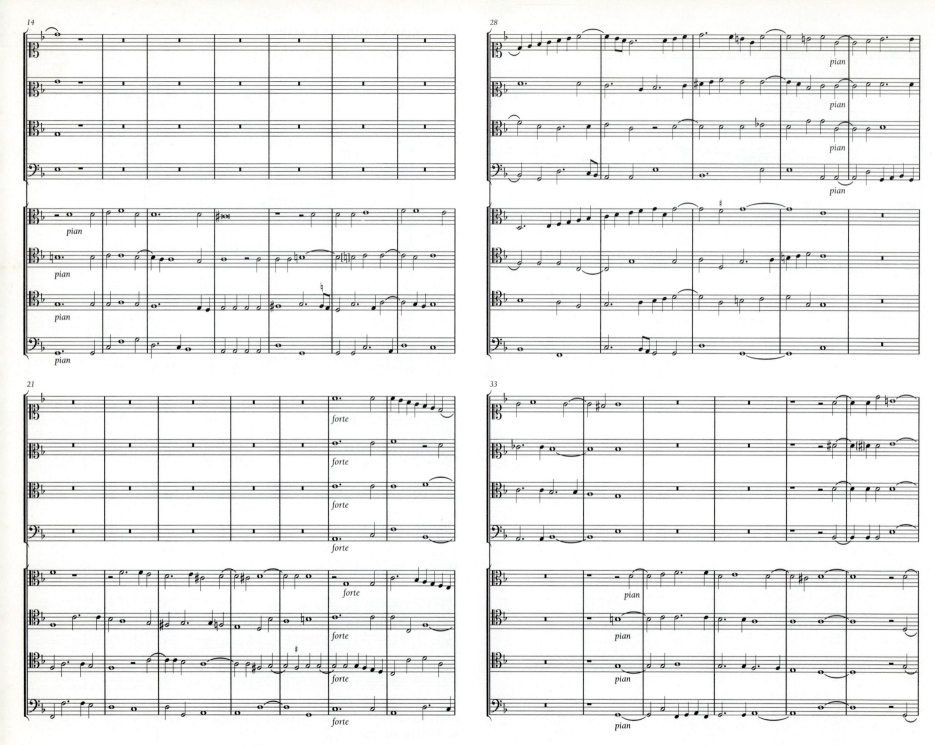

134

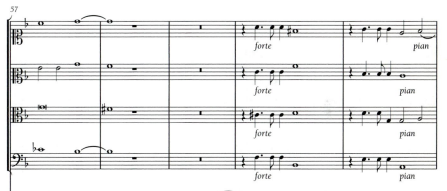

82 **Excerpt from GAUDE DEI GENITRIX, Versets on the Sequence**

Arnolt Schlick (c. 1460–c. 1522)

Gau - de De - i ge - ni - trix, quam circumstant ob - ste - tri - cum vi - ce con - ci - nentes ange - li glori - am De - o.

I **Bassus et discantus in decimis**

Gau - de De - i ge - ni - trix,

quam cir - cum - stant ob - ste - tri - cum

vi - ce con - ci - nen - tes an -

ge - li glo - ri - am De - o.

II **Discantus ex bassu in decimis**
Vagans ex tenore in quartis

Gau - de De - i ge - ni - trix,

quam cir - cum - stant ob - ste - tri - cum

vi - ce con - ci - nen - tes an -

ge - li glo - ri - am De - o.

See DWM p. 218.

Discantus ex tenore in sextis
Vagans ex bassu in tertiis

RECERCAR QUARTO
Girolamo Cavazzoni (c. 1525–c. 1578)

Gau - de De - i ge - ni - trix,

quam cir - cum - stant ob - ste - tri - cum

vi - ce con - ci - nen - tes an -

ge - li glo - ri - am De - o.

See DWM p. 219.

LA STRADA, Canzona

Tarquinio Merula (c. 1594–1665)

See DWM p. 219.

85 IN NOMINE

a Gloria tibi trinitas

Anonymous Sarum Chant

Glo - ri - a ti - bi tri - ni - tas ae - qua - lis, u - na De - i - tas et

an - te om - ni - a sae - cu - la, et nunc, et in per - pe - tu - um.

b IN NOMINE XII: Crye

Christopher Tye (c. 1505–c. 1572)

See DWM pp. 199, 219.

142

DIFERENCIAS SOBRE EL CANTO LLANO DEL CABALLERO

Antonio de Cabezón (1510–1566)

See DWM p. 221.

87 EL MAESTRO: FANTASIA NO. 17

Luys de Milán (c. 1500–1561)

See DWM p. 222.

Girolamo Diruta (c. 1554–c. 1611)

See DWM p. 223.

89

IN ECCLESIIS

Giovanni Gabrieli (c. 1553–1612)

See DWM p. 224.

num. Al - le - lu - ja, [al - le - lu -

[Al - le - lu - ja, al - le - lu - ja,]

[Al - le - lu - ja, al - le - lu - ja,

[Al - le - lu - ja, al - le - lu - ja,]

[Al - le - lu - ja, al - le - lu - ja,]

ja, al - le - lu - ja.]

al - le - lu - ja.

al - le - lu - ja.]

al - le - lu - ja.

al - le - lu - ja.

Sinfonia

Sinfonia

Sinfonia

Sinfonia

Sinfonia

in-vo-ca-mus,]   te _____ a-do-ra   -   mus,

[te   a - do - ra - mus.]   Li - be - ra

[te lau - da-mus,]   te   a-do - ra   -   mus,   [te ____

__   a - do - ra   -   mus.]

In ecclesiis benedicite Domino.
Alleluja.

In omni loco dominationis,
  benedic anima mea Dominum.
Alleluja.

In Deo salutari meo, et gloria mea.
Deus auxilium meum et spes mea in
  Deo est.
Alleluja.

Deus noster, te invocamus,
  te laudamus, te adoramus.
Libera nos, salva nos, vivifica nos.
Alleluja.

Deus, adjutor noster in aeternum.
Alleluja.

In the congregations, bless the Lord.
Alleluia.

In every place in the dominion,
  bless the Lord, [O] my soul.
Alleluia.

In God [is] my salvation, and my glory.
God [is] my help and my hope is in
  God.
Alleluia.

Our God, we invoke Thee,
  we praise Thee, we worship Thee.
Deliver us, save us, give us life.
Alleluia.

God, our helper in eternity.
Alleluia.

AMARILLI MIA BELLA, Madrigal

Giulio Caccini (c. 1545–1618)

*The realization is after Robert Dowland's (1610).

See DWM p. 235.

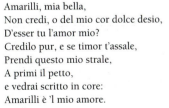

Amarilli, mia bella,
Non credi, o del mio cor dolce desio,
D'esser tu l'amor mio?
Credilo pur, e se timor t'assale,
Prendi questo mio strale,
A primi il petto,
e vedrai scritto in core:
Amarilli è 'l mio amore.

Amarillis, my beautiful one,
Do you not believe, oh, my heart's sweet desire,
that you are my love?
Believe it, by all means! and if fear assails you,
Take this, my arrow,
Open [my] breast,
and you will see written on [my] heart:
"Amaryllis is my love."

91 DAFNE, "Bella ninfa fuggitiva," Chorus

Jacopo Corsi (1561–1602)

Bella ninfa fuggitiva,
Sciolt' e priva
Del mortal tuo nobil velo,
Godi pur pianta novella,
Casta e bella,
Car' al mondo, e car' al cielo.

Beautiful fugitive nymph,
free and deprived
of your noble mortal veil (i.e., form),
enjoy, too, the sad tale,
[you who are] chaste and beautiful,
dear to the world, and dear to the heavens.

(continued)

See DWM p. 239.

Tu non curi e nembi e tuoni:
Tu coroni
Cigni, regi, e dèi celesti:
Geli il cielo o 'nfiammi e scaldi,

Di smeraldi
Lieta ogn' or t'adorni e vesti.

You do not heed either clouds or thunder:
You crown
swans, kings, and heavenly gods:
whether the sky is frosty or inflamed and
    warm,
with emeralds
you, rejoicing, clothe and adorn yourself
    constantly.

Godi pur de' doni egregi;
I tuoi pregi
Non t'invidio e non desio:
Io, se mai d'amor m'assale
Aureo strale
Non vo' guerra con un Dio.

Enjoy, too, the noble gifts;
your treasures
I do not envy you and I do not desire [them];
I, if ever I am assailed by love's
golden arrow,
do not want to fight a god.

Se a fuggir movo le piante
Vero amante,
Contra amor cruda e superba,
Venir possa il mio crin d'auro
Non pur lauro,
Ma qual è più miser' erba.

If I must die to flee the plaint
of a true lover,
against love cruel and proud,
may my golden hair not become
pure (i.e., chaste) laurel,
but that which is a much more lowly plant.

Sia vil canna, il mio crin biondo
Che l'immondo
Gregge ogn' or schianti e dirame;
Sia vil fien, ch'a i crudi denti

De gli armenti
Tragga ogn' or l'avida fame.

May my blond hair be a cheap [i.e., lowly] reed
that the grimy
flock [or, herd] snaps off and prunes every day;
may it be hay of little worth, that, with cruel
    teeth,
the greedy appetites of the herds
pull up every day.

Ma s' a' preghi sospirosi
Amorosi,
Di pietà sfavillo et ardo,
S'io prometto a l'altrui pene
Dolce spene
Con un riso e con un guardo,

But if, with sighing, prayers,
loving,
with compassion, I glow and I burn,
If I promise for another's suffering
sweet hope
with a laugh and with a glance.

Non soffrir, cortese Amore,
Che 'l mio ardore
Prenda a scherno alma gelata;

Non soffrir ch' in piaggia o 'n lido

Cor infido
M'abbandoni innamorata.

Do not grieve, kind Love,
because my ardor
holds in scorn [i.e., is not repelled by] a cold
    spirit;
do not grieve because on the slopes or on the
    shore
unfaithful heart
[my] beloved abandons me.

Fa' ch' al foco de' miei lumi
Si consumi
Ogni gelo, ogni durezza;
Ardi poi quest' alma allora
Ch' altra adora,
Qual si sia la mia bellezza.

—Ottavio Rinuccini

By the fire of my eyes cause
to be dissipated
every chill, every difficulty;
then warm this sweet laurel tree
that adores another,
so that that beautiful one may be mine.

CRUDA AMARILLI, Madrigal

Claudio Monteverdi (1567–1643)

See DWM pp. 245, 247.

Cruda Amarilli, che col nome ancora
D'amar, ahi lasso, amaramente insegni,
Amarilli del candido ligustro
Più candida e più bella,
Ma dell'Aspido sordo
E più sorda e più fera e più fugace,
Poi che col dir t'offendo,
I mi morrò tacendo.

Cruel Amaryllis, who by the name alone,
alas, teaches me to love bitterly.
Amaryllis, purer and more beautiful
than the white privet,
But more callous than the insensitive asp,
more savage and more elusive,
Since I offend you merely by speaking
I will die in silence.

   —G. B. Guarini, from *Il pastor fido*, Act I, scene 2

*Guarini's poem contains puns that translation into English cannot duplicate effectively, e.g., amare (to love), amara (bitter), and Amarilli (lily of love). Amaryllis was the conventional name for a shepherdess in pastoral poetry.

93   L'ORFEO, Act III, "Possente spirto"

Claudio Monteverdi (1567–1643)

*Orfeo al suono del Organo di legno, et un Chitairone, canta una sola de le due parti.**

*Accompanied by wood organ and a chitarrone, Orpheus sings only one of the two parts (preferably the ornamented one).

See DWM p. 248.

Furno sonate le altre parti da tre Viole da braccio, et un contrabasso de Viola tocchi pian piano.

*For the accompaniment, the three viole da braccio and one contrabass viol play very softly.

ORFEO:
Possente Spirto e formidabil Nume
Senza cui far passaggio à l'altra riva
Alma da corpo sciolta in van presume.

INSTRUMENTAL RITORNELLO

Non viv' io, nò, che poi di vita è priva
Mia cara sposa il cor non è più meco,

E senza cor com' esser può ch'io viva?

INSTRUMENTAL RITORNELLO

A lei volt' hò il camin per l'aer cieco,

A l'Inferno non già, ch'ovunque stassi
Tanta bellezza il Paradiso hà seco.

INSTRUMENTAL RITORNELLO

Orfeo son io, che d'Euridice i passi
Seguo per queste tenebrose arene,
Dove giamai per huom mortal non vassi.
O de le luci mie luci serene,
S'un vostro sguardo può tornarmi in vita,
Ahi chi nega il conforto a le mie pene?
Sol tu nobile Dio puoi darmi aita
Né temer dei, che sopra un'aurea Cetra
Sol di corde soavi armo le dita,
Contra cui rigid' alma in van s'impetra.

CARONTE:
Ben solletica alquanto
Dilettandomi il core
Sconsolato Cantore,
Il tuo pianto e'l tuo canto.
Ma lunge, ah lunge sia da questo petto,
Pietà, di mio valor non degno affetto.

ORFEO:
Ahi sventurato amante,
Sperar dunque non lice
Ch' odan miei preghi i Cittadin
    d'Averno?
Onde qual ombra errante
d'insepolto cadavero infelice,
Privo sarò del Cielo e de l'Inferno?

ORPHEUS:
Powerful spirit and formidable god,
without whom souls released from the body
presume in vain to cross to the other bank.

I am not alive, no, since my dear wife
was deprived of life, [my] heart is no longer
    with me,
and without a heart how is it possible for me
    to live?

To her have I turned [my] way through the
    dark air,
not already to Hades, but wherever
so much beauty is, paradise is with her.

I am Orfeo, who follows Euridice's steps
through these dark arenas
where mortal man never has access.
O, serene lights of my lights [= eyes],
if one of your glances is able to restore life,
oh, who denies solace to my distress?
You alone, noble god, can give [me] aid,
do not fear the gods, since [my] fingers
over the sweet strings of a golden lyre
are [my] only weapon against the stern souls
    to whom entreaty is in vain.

CHARON:
I am much flattered by such
delight to my heart,
disconsolate singer,
by your lament and by your song.
But far, ah, far from my breast
is pity, which is beneath my dignity.

ORPHEUS:
Alas, unhappy lover [that I am],
that I am not allowed to hope
that the citizens of Hades will not listen to my
    pleas?
Must I, therefore, like an errant shadow
of an unburied and unhappy corpse,
be deprived of heaven and of hell?

Così vuol empia sorte
Ch'in questi orror di morte
Da te mio cor, lontano
Chiami tuo nome in vano,
E pregando, e piangendo io mi consumi?
Rendetemi'l mio ben Tartarei Numit.

—A. Striggio

Does impious fate will it thus
that I, in this horror of death
far from you, my beloved,
call your name in vain
and consume myself in imploring and weeping?
Give me back my love, gods of Hell.

94 LA GRISELDA, Act II, Scene 4

Alessandro Scarlatti (1660–1725)

From the publishers of *The Operas of Alessandro Scarlatti Volume 3, Griselda,* edited by Donald J. Grout, Cambridge, Massachusetts. Harvard University Press, Copyright © 1975 by the President and Fellows of Harvard College. Reprinted by permission.

See DWM p. 255.

(In-giu-sto pa-dre!) E già e-se-gui-sco la cru-del sen - ten-za che tu stes-sa con-fer-mi.

Io? Sì, col tuo ri - fiu-to. Nè ti mo-ve il mio pianto? Lo be-va-no le a-re-ne.

Nè ti ren-di a' miei prie-ghi? Li di-sper-da-no i ven-ti. Nè t'ap-pa-ga il mio san-gue? Io vo-glio quel-lo

che scor-re nel-le ve-ne al tuo E-ve-rar-do. Gual-tier? Que-sta è sua leg-ge. Ot-ton? Sia-ne il mi -

ni-stro. Il Ciel? Non ti di-fen-de. Il Nu-me? È sor-do. E con dar-ti la de-stra . . .

Puoi ma-dre sal-var il fi-glio, spo-sa pla-car l'a-man-te,, e la man di-sar-mar del fer-ro i-

Gli lascia il fanciullo e parte risoluta.
Poi nell'entrare si ferma alle voci d'Ottone, che stara in atto di ferire Everardo.

gnu-do. Ub-bi-di-sci, ub-bi - di-sci, o cru-del, sve-na-lo, sve-na-lo, o cru-do!

Ma-dre di sas-so: ve - dì, ve - di con quan-ta rab-bia nel-le vi-sce-re tue la spa-da im-mer-go,

ec-co che io già fe - ri-sco. Ahi, che m'ar-re-sta il do-lor, lo spa-ven-to, e fug-gir se-mi-

torna indietro

vi - va in dar-no io ten - to dal-la tra - ge-dia or-ri - bi-le e fu-ne - sta.

Aria

Andante moderato

Violino I

Violino II

Viola

GRISELDA — or all'uno or all'altro

Fi - glio! Ti-

Continuo — solo

178

179

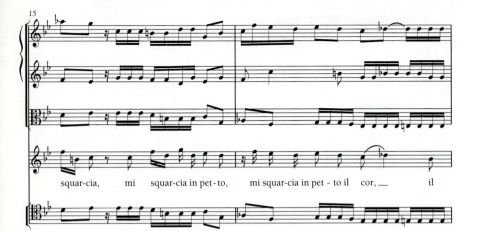

squar-cia, mi squar-cia in pet-to, mi squar-cia in pet - to il cor, — il

cor, — ma il cor trop-po co-stan-te co-sì squar-cia - to an-cor, co-sì squar-cia - to an-

corvin - ce, vin - ce, vin - ce il suo af-fan - no, vin-ce il suo af-fan - no.

Da capo

GRISELDA:
Figlio, figlio, dove t'ascondo da un genitore ingrato che l'immagine sua nel tuo bel viso e ne' tuoi dolci amori, la memoria di me distrugger tenta?

OTTONE:
Nè tutta ancor sai la tua sorte, o donna.

GRISELDA:
Non attendo d'Ottone altro che mali. Che arrechi?

OTTONE:
In questo ferro d'Everardo la morte.

GRISELDA:
(Alma mia, se resisti al tuo dolor sei stupida e non forte.)

OTTONE (ad uno dei seguaci):
Vieni Araspe e m'ascolta, poichè col ferro aperta da più strade a quell' alma avrò l'uscita; tu il cadavere informe in più parti diviso, tenero e poco cibo, gitta alle belve ove più il bosco annotta.

GRISELDA:
Ah, Ottone . . .

OTTONE:
In van contrasti.

GRISELDA:
Pargoletto infelice, in che peccasti?

OTTONE (ai soldati):
Appressatevi.

GRISELDA (in atto di prostrarsi):
Ah Prence . . .

OTTONE:
Donna, che chiedi?

GRISELDA:
È madre quella che a te s'inchina e umil ti priego.

GRISELDA:
Son, son, where do I hide you from an ungrateful father who is trying to destroy his own likeness in your handsome face, and in your sweet love, the memory of me?

OTTONE:
You do not yet know all of your fate, O woman.

GRISELDA:
I do not expect from Ottone anything but evil. What do you bring?

OTTONE:
In this sword, death for Everardo.

GRISELDA:
(My soul, if you resist in your grief you are stupid and not strong.)

OTTONE (to one of his followers):
Come, Araspe, and listen to me. After you have opened the way out for this soul, by several paths, with the sword, cut the shapeless corpse into many pieces, [as] tender little bits of food, and cast [them] to the wild beasts where the woods are darkest.

GRISELDA:
Ah, Ottone . . .

OTTONE:
In vain you resist.

GRISELDA:
Unfortunate baby, in what have you sinned?

OTTONE (to the soldiers):
Draw near.

GRISELDA (prostrating herself):
Ah, Prince . . .

OTTONE:
Woman, what do you ask?

GRISELDA:
The woman who bows before you and humbly begs you is a mother.

OTTONE:
A chi niega pietà pietà si niega.

GRISELDA:
Lasciami il caro figlio e se io t'offesi prendi in me la tua vittima.

OTTONE:
Risolvi: o mi sposa, o l'uccido.

GRISELDA (osservando il fanciullo):
Il misero innocente tien fisse in me le pupillette e nulla sa della sua sciagura.

OTTONE:
Griselda, se più tardi non sei più madre, io già misuro il colpo che Gualtiero m'impose.

GRISELDA:
(Ingiusto padre!)

OTTONE:
E già eseguisco la crudel sentenza che tu stessa confermi.

GRISELDA:
Io?

OTTONE:
Sì, col tuo rifiuto.

GRISELDA:
Nè ti move il mio pianto?

OTTONE:
Lo bevano le arene.

GRISELDA:
Nè ti rendi a' miei prieghi?

OTTONE:
Li disperdano i venti.

GRISELDA:
Nè t'appaga il mio sangue?

OTTONE:
Io voglio quello che scorre nelle vene al tuo Everardo.

OTTONE:
To the one who denies pity, pity is denied.

GRISELDA:
Leave me my dear son, and if I have offended you, take me as your victim.

OTTONE:
Decide: either marry me, or I will kill him.

GRISELDA (looking at the little boy):
The unfortunate innocent one keeps his little eyes fixed on me and knows nothing of his misfortune.

OTTONE:
Griselda, if you delay longer, you will no longer be a mother; I am already measuring the blow that Gualtiero imposed on me.

GRISELDA:
(Unjust father!)

OTTONE:
And already I am carrying out the cruel sentence that you yourself confirm.

GRISELDA:
I?

OTTONE:
Yes, with your refusal.

GRISELDA:
Don't my tears move you?

OTTONE:
Let the soil drink them.

GRISELDA:
Nor do my prayers move you?

OTTONE:
Let the winds scatter them.

GRISELDA:
Nor does my blood appease you?

OTTONE:
I want that which flows in the veins of your Everardo.

GRISELDA:
Gualtier?

OTTONE:
Questa è sua legge.

GRISELDA:
Otton?

OTTONE:
Siane il ministro.

GRISELDA:
Il Ciel?

OTTONE:
Non ti difende.

GRISELDA:
Il Nume?

OTTONE:
È sordo.

GRISELDA:
E con darti la destra . . .

OTTONE:
Puoi madre salvar il figlio, sposa placar l'amante, e la man disarmar del ferro ignudo.

GRISELDA:
Ubbidisci, ubbidisci, o crudel, svenalo, svenalo, o crudo!

(Gli lascia il fanciullo e parte risoluta. Poi nell' entrare si ferma alle voci d'Ottone, che stara in atto di ferire Everardo.)

OTTONE:
Madre di sasso: vedi, vedi con quanta rabbia nelle viscere tue la spada immergo, ecco che io già ferisco.

GRISELDA:
Ahi, che m'arresta il dolor, lo spavento, e fuggir semiviva indarno io tento dalla tragedia orribile e funesta.

GRISELDA:
Gualtiero?

OTTONE:
This is his order.

GRISELDA:
Ottone?

OTTONE:
Is to be his minister.

GRISELDA:
Heaven?

OTTONE:
Does not defend you.

GRISELDA:
God?

OTTONE:
Is deaf.

GRISELDA:
And by giving my hand . . .

OTTONE:
The mother can save her son, the bride can appease her lover, and can disarm the hand of the unsheathed sword.

GRISELDA:
Obey, obey, O cruel man, kill him, let him bleed to death, O cruel man!

(She leaves the child and resolutely starts to leave. As she is about to go, Ottone's voice stops her; he is in the act of stabbing Everardo.)

OTTONE:
Mother of stone: see, see with how much rage I plunge the blade into your viscera; behold that already I am striking.

GRISELDA:
Alas, that the grief stops me, the fright, and in vain I try, half alive, to flee from the horrible and fatal tragedy.

Figlio! Tiranno! O Dio!
Dite che far poss' io, che?
O Dio! Figlio
Che far poss' io?
Figlio! Tirrano!
(Fine)

L'amor di madre amante
mi squarcia in petto il cor,
ma il cor troppo costante
così squarciato ancor,
vince il suo affanno.
(Da capo al Fine)

ARIA

Son! Tyrant! O God!
Tell me, what can I do, what?
O God! Son
What can I do?
Son! Tyrant!
(Fine)

The love of a loving mother
tears my heart in my breast,
but the steadfast heart
even so torn apart,
overcomes its suffering.
(Da capo al Fine)

95 ALCESTE, Ouverture
Jean-Baptiste Lully (1632–1687)

See DWM p. 258.

DIDO AND AENEAS, Act III, Dido: Recitative—Aria,
"Thy hand, Belinda"—"When I am laid in earth"—Chorus,
"With drooping wings"

Henry Purcell (1659–1695)

See DWM p. 259

97 JEPHTE, Conclusion, Oratorio

Giacomo Carissimi (1605–1674)

See DWM p. 262.

HISTORICUS:
Cum vidisset Jephte qui votum Domino
   voverat
filiam suam venientem in occursum,
in dolore et lacrimis scidit vestimenta sua
   et ait:

JEPHTE:
Heu, heu mihi filia mea,
heu! decepisti me filia unigenita,
decepisti me, et tu pariter.
Heu, filia mea, decepta es,
   decepta es.

FILIA:
Cur ego te pater decepi
et cur ego filia tua unigenita decepta
   sum?

JEPHTE:
Aperui os meum ad Dominum
ut quicumque primus de domo mea occurrerit
   mihi
offeram illum Dominum in holocaustum.
Heu mihi filia mea,
heu! decepisti me filia unigenita,
decepisti me et tu pariter
heu! filia mea decepta es, decepta es.

FILIA:
Pater mi, pater mi,
si vovisti votum Domino,
reversus victor ab hostibus,
ecce ego filia tua unigenita
offer me in holocaustum victoriae tuae
hoc solum, pater mi
praesta filiae tuae unigenitae ante quam moriar.

JEPHTE:
Quid poterit animam tuam,
quid poterit te moritura filia consolari?

FILIA:
Dimitte me ut duobus mensibus circumeam
   montes,
ut cum sodalibus meis plangam,
plangam virginitatem meam.

JEPHTE:
Vade filia, vade filia mea unigenita
et plange, et plange virginitatem tuam.

NARRATOR:
When Jephta realized that he had promised to
   God
his daughter who came running to meet him,
in sorrow and tears
he tore his clothing and said:

JEPHTA:
Alas, woe to me, my daughter,
Alas! you have brought me low, [my] only child,
you have victimized me and yourself equally.
Alas, my daughter, you have been brought low,
   you have been victimized.

DAUGHTER:
How have I brought you low, father,
and how have I, your only child, been victimized?

JEPHTA:
I have opened my mouth to God
that whatever first came running to meet me
   from my house
I would offer that to God as burnt offering.
Woe to me, my daughter,
Alas! you have brought me low, only child,
you have victimized me and yourself equally.
Alas! my daughter, you have been brought low,
   you have been victimized.

DAUGHTER:
My father, my father,
if you have vowed a vow to God,
having returned victor over the enemy,
behold, I, your only-begotten child,
offer me as burnt offering for your victory.
Only this one thing, my father,
grant to your only-begotten child before I die.

JEPHTA:
What could console your spirit,
what could comfort you, daughter about to die?

DAUGHTER:
Let me go away for two months to walk about
   in the mountains,
so that I, with my companions, may bewail,
bewail loudly, my virginity.*

JEPHTA:
Go, daughter, go, my only-begotten child,
and weep, and bewail your virginity.

HISTORICUS—CHORUS:
Abiit ergo in montes filia Jephte
et plorabat cum sodalibus virginitatem
   suam
dicens:

FILIA:
Plorate, plorate colles,
dolete, dolete montes,
et in afflictione cordis mei ululate,
et in afflictionis cordis mei ululate.

ECO: Ululate.

FILIA:
Ecce nunc moriar virgo
et non potero morte mea meis filiis
   consolari—
ingemiscite silvae, fontes, et flumina
in interitu virginis lacrimate,
fontes et flumina in interitu virginis lacrimate.—

ECO: Lacrimate.

FILIA:
Heu me dolentem,
heu me dolentem in laetitia populi

in victoria Israel et gloria patris mei
ego sine filiis virgo
ego filia unigenita moriar et non vivam!
Exhorrescite rupes,
obstupescite colles,
valles et cavernae in sonitu horribili,
resonate, valles et cavernae in sonitu
   horribili,
in sonitu horribili, resonate!

ECO: Resonate!

FILIA:
Plorate, plorate filii Israel,
plorate virginitatem meam
et Jephte filiam unigenitam in carmina doloris
   lamentamini,
et Jephte filiam unigenitam in carmine doloris
   lamentamini.

HISTORICUS, with CHORUS:
Therefore, Jephta's daughter went away into
   the mountains
and, with her companions, bewailed her virginity,
saying:

DAUGHTER:
Weep, weep, little hills,
Grieve, grieve, mountains,
and wail loudly for my heartfelt affliction,
and caterwaul for my heartfelt affliction.

ECHO: Caterwaul.

DAUGHTER:
Behold, now, I am to die a virgin
and in my death** I will not be able to be con-
   soled by my children—
Groan and sigh, forests, fountains, and rivers,
weep for a virgin's annihilation,
fountains and streams, for a virgin's sacrifice,
   weep.

ECHO: Weep!

DAUGHTER:
Woe, for my sorrowing,
Alas, for my grieving, in the unrestrained gladness of the people
in Israel's victory and my father's glory,
I, a virgin, childless,
I, only-begotten daughter, to die and not live!
Shudder exceedingly, rocky cliffs,
Be astounded, little hills,
valleys and caverns, with horrible noises,
resound, valleys and caverns, with frightful
   sounds,
with horrible sounds, resound!

ECHO: Resound!

DAUGHTER:
Weep, weep, Israeli children,
bewail my virginity
and lament Jephta's only-begotten child in
   songs of sorrow,
and lament Jephta's only-begotten child in
   songs of sorrow.

194

CHORUS:

Plorate filii Israel,

plorate omnes virginem et filiam Jephte
  unigenitam,

in carmine doloris, lamentamini, lamentamini, lamentamini.

(Stanza of text is repeated)

CHORUS:

Mourn, Israeli children,

All mourn the virgin and Jephta's
  only child,

in songs of sorrow, lament,
  wail, weep.

*bewail the fact that she will die a virgin,
  childless.

**that she does not have children to comfort
  her in the hour of her death.

98   SYMPHONIAE SACRAE, Motet 9

O quam tu pulchra es, amica mea

Heinrich Schütz (1585–1672)

See DWM p. 265.

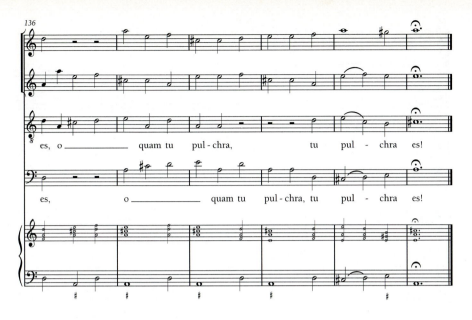

O quam tu pulchra, es, amica mea,
columba mea, formosa mea, immaculata mea!
Oculi tui, oculi columbarum.
O quam tu pulchra es!
Capilli tui sicut greges caprarum.
O quam tu pulchra es!
Dentos tui sicut greges tonsarum.
O quam tu pulchra es!
Sicut vitta coccinea labia tua.

O quam tu pulchra es!
Sicut turris David collum, collum tuum.
O quam tu pulchra es!
Duo ubera tua sicut duo hinnuli,
sicut duo hinnuli capreae gemelli.
O quam tu pulchra es!

O, how beautiful you are, my friend,
my dove, my beauty, my undefiled one!
Your eyes, the eyes of a dove.
O, how beautiful you are!
Your hair is like a flock of she-goats.
O, how beautiful you are!
Your teeth are like a flock of [ewes] newly-shorn.
O, how beautiful you are!
Your lips are as scarlet as the ribbon headband
    worn by sacrificial victims.
O, how beautiful you are!
Your neck is like the tower of David.
O, how beautiful you are!
Your two breasts are like two young fawns,
like two twin fawns that are roe deer.
O, how beautiful you are!

99 DIE SIEBEN WORTE . . . JESU CHRISTI AM KREUZ, Introit

Heinrich Schütz (1585–1672)

See DWM p. 266.

Da Jesus an dem Kreuze stund
und ihm sein Leichnam war verwundt,
so gar mit bitterm Schmerzen,
die sieben Wort, die Jesus sprach,
betracht in deinem Herzen,

While Jesus stood on the cross,
and his body was wounded,
even in bitter pain,
the seven words that Jesus spoke,
consider in your heart.

100 FANTASIA CHROMATICA

Jan Pieterzoon Sweelinck (1562–1621)

See DWM pp. 270, 276.

201

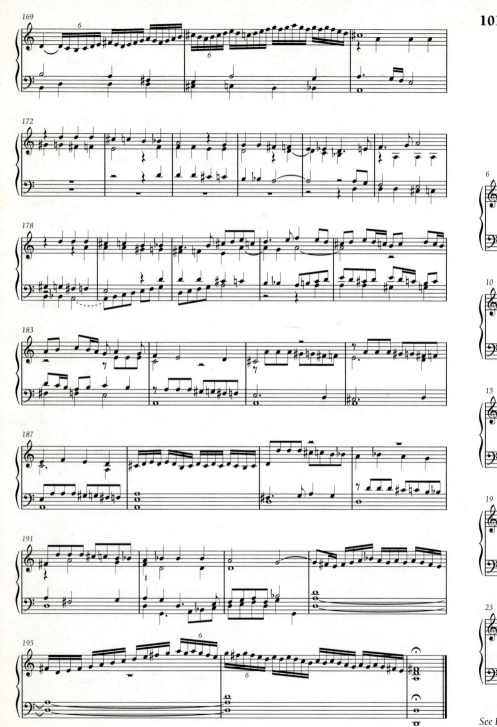

101 CANZONA PER L'EPISTOLA

Anonymous

See DWM p. 271.

102 SUITE XXII, in E minor

Johann Froberger (1616–1667)

Allemande

See DWM p. 273.

205

103 TOCCATA NONA, from IL SECONDO LIBRO DI TOCCATE

Girolamo Frescobaldi (1583–1643)

See DWM pp. 274, 278.

Non senza fatiga
si giunge al fine.

104   VATER UNSER IM HIMMELREICH, Chorale Preludes

a   Samuel Scheidt (1587–1654)

b   Dietrich Buxtehude (c. 1637–1707)

See DWM p. 277.

c   **Johann Pachelbel (1653–1706)**

d **Johann Sebastian Bach (1685–1750)**

105 MESSA DELLA MADONNA, RICERCAR DOPO IL CREDO

Girolamo Frescobaldi (1583–1643)

See DWM p. 279.

Elisabeth-Claude Jacquet de la Guerre (c. 1666–1729)

La Flamande

From Elisabeth Jacquet de la Guerre: *Pièces de clavecin* Ed. Paul Brunold, Editions de l'Oiseau-Lyre Monaco 1965.

See DWM p. 282.

Courante

Double

Sarabande

[𝄐] 2ᵉ fois

Gigue

Double

217

2me Gigue

218

107 VINGT-CINQUIÈME ORDRE

François Couperin (1668–1733)

a   La Visionaire

See DWM p. 282.

b   La Misterieuse

Modérément

Reprise

c **La Monflambert**

d **La Muse victorieuse**

e   Les Ombres errantes

Languissamment

222

108 SONATA DA CAMERA, Op. 2, No. 4

Arcangelo Corelli (1653–1713)

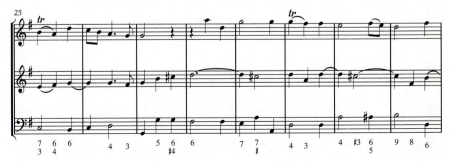

See DWM p. 293.

Allemanda

Grave   Adagio

Giga

Arcangelo Corelli (1653–1713)

Corelli's Graces

Grave

Violino solo

Violone
e Cimbalo

Allegro

Tasto solo

Adagio

See DWM pp. 290, 293.

228

110 CONCERTO IN A MAJOR, for Violin and Orchestra, Op. 9, No. 2, mvts. 1, 2

Antonio Vivaldi (1678–1741)

© 1998 by A-R Editions, Inc. Used with permission.

See DWM pp. 301, 302.

233

234

Georg Philipp Telemann (1681–1767)

See DWM p. 304.

Da capo al Fine

240

112 CASTOR ET POLLUX,
Act IV, Scene 1, "Séjour de l'éternelle paix"

Jean-Philippe Rameau (1683–1764)

Le théâtre représente les Champs-Elysées; diverses troupes d'Ombres heureuses paraissent dans l'éloignement.

Scène I. CASTOR

Sé - jour de l'é-ter-nel-le paix, Ne cal-me-rez-vous point _____ mon

See DWM p. 307.

ARIA:

Séjour de l'éternelle paix,
Ne calmerez-vous point mon âme impatiente?

RECITATIF:

Temple des demi dieux que j'habite à jamais,
Combattez dans mon coeur ma flamme renais-
    sante!
L'amour jusqu'en ces lieux me poursuit de ses
    traits.
Castor n'y voit que son amante,
Et vous perdez tous vos attraits.

ARIA:

Séjour de l'éternelle paix,
Ne calmerez-vous point mon âme impatiente?

Que ce murmure est doux,
Que cet ombrage est frais!
De ces accords touchants la volupte
    m'enchante!
Tout rit, tout prévient mon attente,
Et je forme encor des regrets!

Séjour de l'éternelle paix,
Ne calmerez-vous point mon âme impatiente?

    —from libretto by P.-J. Bernard

ARIA:

Abode of eternal peace,
Will you not calm my impatient soul at all?

RECITATIVE:

Temple of the demigods that I inhabit forever,
Combat in my heart my reborn passion!

Love, even to these places, pursues me with his
    darts.
Castor sees only his beloved there,
And you lose all your attractions.

ARIA:

Abode of eternal peace,
Will you not calm my impatient soul at all?

How sweet this murmur is!
How cool this shade is!
The voluptuousness of these touching harmonies
    enchants me!
All is favorable, everything forestalls my yearning,
And still I have some regrets!

Abode of eternal peace,
Will you not calm my impatient soul at all?

113   L'ENHARMONIQUE, Clavecin Piece

Jean-Philippe Rameau (1683–1764)

See DWM p. 307.

114 EIN' FESTE BURG IST UNSER GOTT,
Cantata No. 80, Mvt. 1

Johann Sebastian Bach (1685–1750)

See DWM p. 312.

(Melodie: "Ein feste Burg")

247

248

264

Ein' feste Burg ist unser Gott,
ein' gute Wehr und Waffen;
er hilft uns frei aus aller Noth

die uns jetzt hat betroffen.

Der alte böse Feind
mit Ernst er's jetzt meint,
gross' Macht und viel' List
sein' grausam' Rüstung ist,
auf Erd' ist nicht sein's Gleichen.

—Martin Luther

A mighty fortress is our God,
a good bulwark and weapon;
He helps extricate us from all trouble
[or, He is our help in every need]
that even now has afflicted us.

The ancient evil foe
earnestly is still of the opinion
[that] great power and much cunning
are his cruel defense;
on earth there is no one his equal.

115 ST. MATTHEW PASSION, Excerpts

Johann Sebastian Bach (1685–1750)

a **Nos. 69–70. "Ach, Golgatha!" Recitative;
"Sehet, Jesus hat die Hand," Aria with Chorus**

See DWM p. 314, and facsimile, plate 19.

RECITATIVO:

Ach, Golgatha, unsel'ges Golgatha!
Der Herr der Herrlichkeit muss schimpflich hier
    verderben,
der Segen und das Heil der Welt
wird als ein Fluch an's Kreuz gestellt.
Der Schöpfer Himmels und der Erden
soll Erd' und Luft entzogen werden;
die Unschuld muss hier schuldig sterben.
Das gehet meiner Seele nah;
Ach, Golgatha, unsel'ges Golgatha!

ARIA CON CORO:

Sehet, Jesus hat die Hand,
uns zu fassen ausgespannt.
Kommt. Wohin? In Jesu Armen.
Sucht Erlösung nehmt Erbarmen,
Suchet! Wo? In Jesu Armen.
Lebet, sterbet, ruhet hier,
ihr verlass'nen Küchlein ihr,
Bleibet. Wo? In Jesu Armen.

RECITATIVE:

Ah, Golgotha, accursed Golgotha!
Here the Lord of heaven must be disgracefully
    killed,
the blessed Saviour of the world
will be hanged on the cross like a malefactor.
The Creator of heaven and earth
shall be deprived of earth and sky; [or, shall perish]
the innocent must die here, as guilty.
That grieves my soul;
Ah, Golgotha, accursed Golgotha!

ARIA WITH CHORUS:

See, Jesus has his hands
outstretched to grasp us.
Come. Where? In Jesus' arms.
Seek redemption, seek mercy,
Seek! Where? In Jesus' arms.
Live, die, rest here,
You forsaken little flock [literally, little chickens],
Stay. Where? In Jesus' arms.

b **No. 73. "Und siehe da, der Vorhang," Recitative;
"Wahrlich, dieser ist Gottes Sohn gewesen," Chorus**

RECITATIVO:
Und siehe da, der Vorhang im Tempel
zerriss in zwei Stück, von oben an bis
unten aus.

Und die Erde erbebete, und die Felsen
zerissen, und die Gräber täten sich
auf, und stunden auf viel Leiber der
Heiligen, die da schliefen; und gingen
aus den Gräbern nach seiner
Auferstehung, und kamen in die
heilige Stadt, und erschienen vielen.

Aber der Hauptmann, und die bei ihm
waren, und bewahreten Jesum, da sie
sahen das Erdbeben, und was da
geschah, erschraken sie sehr, und
sprachen:

CORO:
Wahrlich, dieser ist Gottes Sohn gewesen.

RECITATIVE:
And behold, the veil [curtain] in the
temple was ripped into two pieces,
from the top to the bottom.

And the earth quaked, and the rocks
split, and the graves opened, and
there arose many bodies of the saints,
who slept there; and they came out of
the graves after his resurrection, and
came into the Holy City, and
appeared to many.

Now, the centurion, and those who were
with him, and watching Jesus, when
they saw the earthquake, and what
happened there, they feared greatly,
and said:

CHORUS:
Truly, this was the Son of God.

116 DAS WOHLTEMPERIRTE KLAVIER [Volume I]: Prelude and Fugue in C Minor, BWV 847

Johann Sebastian Bach (1685–1750)

a Prelude

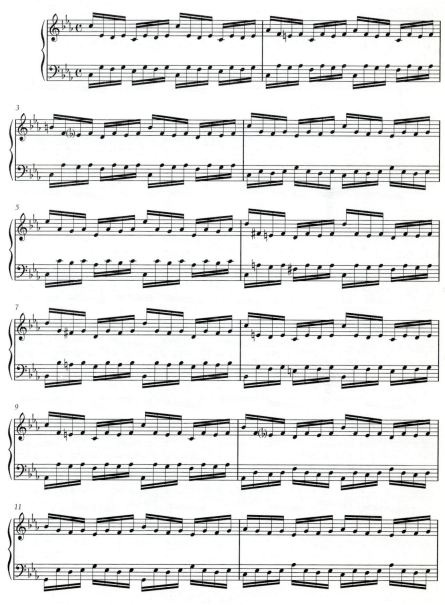

See DWM p. 317.

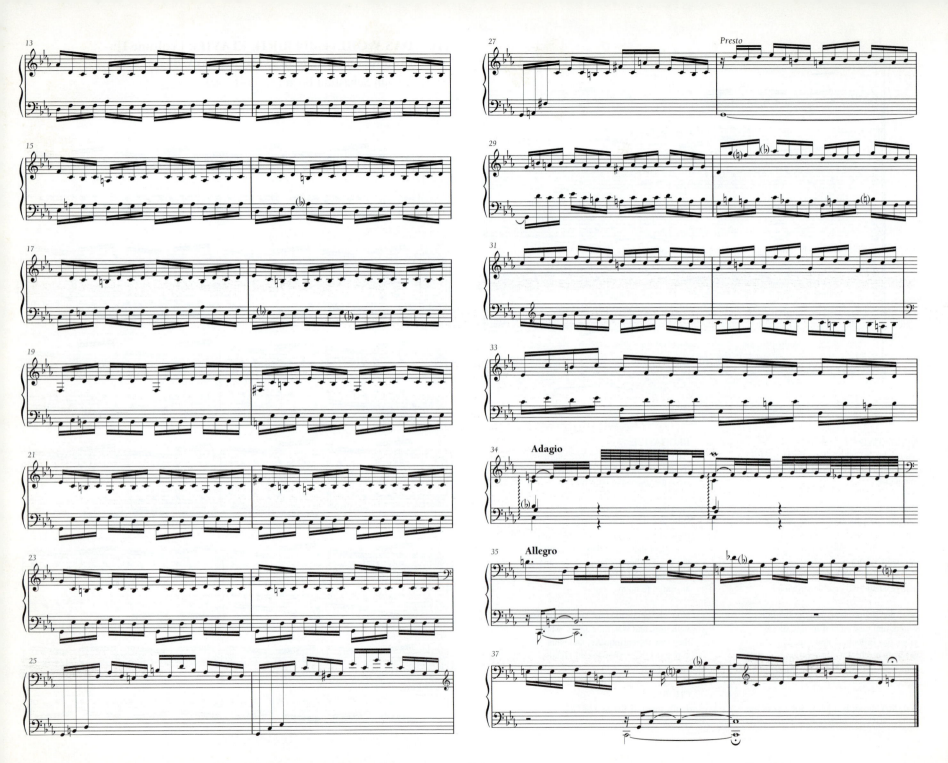

b   Fugue

117 DURCH ADAMS FALL IST GANZ VERDERBT, BMV 637, Chorale Prelude

Johann Sebastian Bach (1685–1750)

See DWM pp. 277, 317.

118 GIULIO CESARE, Act III, Scene 7

George Frideric Handel (1685–1759)

Appartamento di Cleopatra

CLEOPATRA (con guardie) frà le sue damigelle, che piangono, e poi CESARE con soldati.

Adagio, e piano

Oboe

Violino 1

Violino 2

Viola

Basso

(Senza oboe)

CLEOPATRA

Voi, che mie fi-de an-cel-le   un tem-po

fo-ste,   or la-gri - ma-te in van,   più mie non sie-te.   Il bar-ba-ro ger-

See DWM p. 324.

Fine

Da Capo al Fine

CLEOPATRA:

Voi, che mie fide ancelle
    un tempo foste,
or lagrimate in van,
più mie non siete.
Il barbaro germano,
che mi privò del regno,
a me vi toglie,
e a me torrà la vita.
Mà qual strepito d'armi?
Ah sì! più mie non siete,
spirar l'alma Cleopatra or or vedrete.

CLEOPATRA:

You, who were my faithful handmaidens,

now weep in vain,
no longer are you mine.
The barbarous brother-german,
who deprived me of my kingdom,
takes you from me, too,
and from me he will take my life.
But that clash of arms?
Ah, yes! No longer are you mine,
now you will see Cleopatra die.

Caesar enters, with his drawn sword in his hand, and with soldiers.

CAESAR:

Forzai l'ingresso a tua salvezza,
    oh cara!

CAESAR:

I forced my way here to rescue you,
    oh beloved!

CLEOPATRA:

Cesare o un'ombra sei?

CLEOPATRA:

Is it Caesar or his ghost?

CAESAR:

Olà, partite omai, empii ministri
    d'un tiranno spietato!
Cesare così vuol, pronti ubbidite!

CAESAR:

Hallo! prison guards, impious servants
    of a ruthless tyrant!
Caesar expects you to obey instantly!

He signals for guards to leave; they do so.

CLEOPATRA:

Ah! ben ti riconosco, amato mio tesoro,
    al valor del tuo braccio!
ombra, nò, tu non sei, Cesare amato!

CLEOPATRA

Ah! now I recognize you, my beloved treasure.
    the strength (valor) of your arms!
A ghost, no, you are not, beloved Caesar!

CAESAR:

Cara! ti stringo al seno;
ha cangiato vicende il nostro fato.

CAESAR:

Beloved! I clasp you to my breast;
our fate is changing.

CLEOPATRA:

Come salvo ti vedo?

CLEOPATRA:

How did you come to safety?

CAESAR:

Tempo avrò di svelarti ogni ascosa
    cagion del viver mio.
Libera sei, vanne frà tanto al porto,
    e le disperse schiere
    in un raduna;
    colà mi rivedrai;
Marte mi chiama all' impresa total di
    questo suolo.
Per conquistar, non che l'Egitto,
    un mondo, basta l'ardir di questo
    petto solo.

CLEOPATRA:

Da tempeste il legno infranto,
se poi salvo giunge in porto,
non sà più che desiar.

Così il cor trà pene e pianto,
or che trova il suo conforto,
torna l'anima a bear.

CAESAR:

Later I will reveal every adventure
    of my life.
You are free, follow me to the harbor,
    the scattered troops have been
    summoned for review,
    which you will do with me;
Mars clearly calls me to his quest,

To complete the conquest not only of Egypt,
    but the whole world and realize my
    ambition.

CLEOPATRA:

Out of the storm, the beaten ship,
if it safely reaches port,
has no further desire.

Thus, the heart torn by pain and weeping,
when it has found comfort,
causes the spirit to rejoice again.

George Frideric Handel (1685–1759)

a   **"Comfort ye," Accompanied Recitative**

Larghetto e piano

senza ripieno   *simile*   *tr*

Violino 1

simile

Violino 2

simile

Viola

Bassi
(Violoncello, Violone,
Cembalo)

simile

Com-fort ye,   com - fort ye   my peo-ple,

com - fort ye,   com - fort ye   my peo-ple,

saith your God,   saith your God.   Speak ye com-fort-a-bly to   Je-

ru - sa-lem,   speak ye com-fort-a-bly to   Je - ru - sa-lem,   and cry un - to her, that her

war - fare,   her war - fare is ac-com-plish'd,   that her in - i - qui-ty   is

See DWM p. 325.

284

b   **"Every valley," Aria**

c   **"And the Glory of the Lord," Chorus**

Appendix A
Names of Instruments and Abbreviations

This table sets forth the English, Italian, German, and French names used in music scores for the various musical instruments, together with their respective abbreviations. Presentation is in the arrangement that has become standard in instrumental scores, reading from the top of the score down: Woodwinds, Brass, Percussion, Strings. Those instruments that are used only occasionally are presented last in this table.

Woodwinds

English	Italian	German	French
Piccolo (Picc.)	Flauto piccolo (Fl. Picc.)	Kleine Flöte (Kl. Fl.)	Petite flûte; Flûte piccolo (Fl. picc.)
Flute (Fl.)	Flauto (Fl.); Flauto grande (Fl. gr.)	Grosse Flöte (Fl. gr.)	Flûte (Fl.)
Alto Flute	Flauto contralto (Fl. c-alto) [pl., Flauti]	Altflöte [pl., Flöten]	Flûte en sol [pl., Flûtes]
Oboe (Ob.)	Oboe (Ob.) [pl., Oboi]	Hoboe (Hb.); Oboe (Ob.) [pl., Hoboen, Oboen]	Hautbois (Hb.) [pl., Hautbois]
English Horn (E. H.)	Corno inglese (C.; C.i.; Cor. ingl.)	Englisches Horn (Englh.; E. H.)	Cor anglais (C. A.)
Sopranino Clarinet	Clarinetto piccolo (Cl. picc.; Clar. picc.)		
Clarinet (C.; Cl.; Clt.; Clar.)	Clarinetto (Cl.; Clar.) [pl., Clarinetti]	Klarinette (Kl.) [pl., Klarinetten]	Clarinette (Cl.) [pl., Clarinettes]
Bass Clarinet (B. Cl.)	Clarinetto basso (Cl. b.; Cl. basso; Clar. basso)	Bassklarinette (Bkl.; Bs. Kl.; B.-Kl.)	Clarinette basse (Cl. bs.)
Bassoon (Bsn.; Bssn.)	Fagotto (Fag.; Fg.)	Fagott (Fag.; Fg.)	Basson (Bssn.)
Contrabassoon (C. Bsn.)	Contrafagotto (Cfg.; C. Fag.; Cont. F.) [pl., Fagotti]	Kontrafagott (Kfg.) [pl., Fagotte]	Contrebasson (C. bssn.; Cbn.) [pl., Bassons]

Brass

English	Italian	German	French
French Horn, or Horn (Hr.; Hn.)	Corno (Cor.; C.) [pl., Corni]	Horn (Hr.) [pl., Hörner (Hrn.)]	Cor; Cor à piston [pl., Cors]
Trumpet (Tpt.; Trpt.; Trp.; Tr.)	Tromba (Tr.) [pl., Trombe]	Trompete (Tr.; Trp.) [pl., Trompeten]	Trompette (Tr.) [pl., Trompettes]

Trombone (Tr.; Tbe.; Trb.; Trbe.; Trm.)	Trombone (Tbn.)
	  [pl., Tromboni (Tbni.; Trni.)]
		Posaune (Ps.; Pos.)
		  [pl., Posaunen]
			Trombone (Trb.)
			  [pl., Trombones]

Tuba (Tb.)	Tuba (Tb.; Tba.)	Tuba (Tb.); Basstuba (Btb.)	Tuba (Tb.)

PERCUSSION

ENGLISH	ITALIAN	GERMAN	FRENCH
Percussion (Perc.)	Percussione	Schlagzeug (Schlag.)	Batterie (Batt.)
Timpani (Timp.); Kettledrums (K. D.)	Timpani (Timp.; Tp.)	Pauken (Pk.)	Timbales (Timb.)

Snare Drum (S. D.)	Tamburo piccolo (Tamb. picc.);
	  Tamburo militare
		Kleine Trommel (Kl. Tr.)	Caisse Claire (C. cl.); Tambour
			  (Militaire) (Tamb. milit.)

Tenor Drum (T. Dr.)	Cassa Rullante	Wirbeltrommel	Caisse Roulante
Bass Drum (B. Dr.)	Gran Cassa (G. C.; Gr. C.; Gr. Cassa)	Grosse Trommel (Gr. Tr.)	Grosse Caisse (Gr. c.)
Cymbals (Cym.; Cymb.)	Piatti (P.; Ptti.; Piat.)	Becken (Beck.)	Cymbales (Cym.)
Tambourine (Tamb.)	Tamburino (Tamb.)	Schellentrommel; Tambourin (Tamb.)	Tambour de Basque (T. de B.; Tamb. de B.; Tamb. de Basque)
Triangle (Trgl.)	Triangolo (Trgl.)	Triangel	Triangle (Triang.)
Tam-tam; Gong (Tam-T.)	Tam-tam	Tam-tam	Tam-tam
Orchestra Bells; Glockenspiel (Glsp.)	Campanelli (Cmp.)	Glockenspiel (Glsp.)	Jeu de Timbres; Carillon
Tubular Bells; Chimes	Campane (Cmp.)	Glocken	Jeu de Cloches; Cloches
Antique Cymbals; Crotales (Crot.)	Piatti antichi; Crotali	Zimbeln; Antiken Zimbeln	Cymbales Antiques; Crotales
Xylophone (Xyl.)	Xilofono	Xylophon	Xylophone (Xyl.)
Siren			Sirène
Cowbells	Cencerro	Kuhlglocken; Herdenglocken	Sonnailles
Wood Blocks (W. Bl.)	Blocco de Legno Cinese	Holzblock	Bloc de Bois
Castanets	Castagnette	Kastagnetten	Castagnettes

STRINGS

ENGLISH	ITALIAN	GERMAN	FRENCH
Violin (V.; Vln.; Vi.)	Violino (V.; Vl.; Vln.)	Violine (V.; Vl.; Vln.); Geige (Gg.)	Violon (V.; Vl.; Vln.)

Viola (Va.; Vl.)
  [pl., Vas.]
	Viola (Va.; Vla.)
	  [pl., Viole (Vle.)]
		Bratsche (Br.)	Alto (A.)

Violoncello; 'Cello (Vcl.; Vc.)	Violoncello (Vc.; Vlc.; Vcllo.)	Violoncell (Vc.; Vlc.)	Violoncelle (Vc.)
Double Bass (D. Bs.)	Contrabasso (Cb.; C.B.) [pl., Contrabassi; Bassi (C. Bassi; Bi.)]	Kontrabass (Kb.)	Contrebasse (C.-B.)

OTHER INSTRUMENTS USED OCCASIONALLY
When included in the orchestra, notation for these instruments is usually placed in the score between percussion and strings.

ENGLISH	ITALIAN	GERMAN	FRENCH
Harp (Hp.; Hrp.)	Arpa (A.; Arp.)	Harfe (Hrf.)	Harpe (Hp.)
Piano (Pno.)	Pianoforte (P-f.; Pft.)	Klavier (Kl.)	Piano
Celeste (Cel.)	Celesta	Celesta	Célesta
Harpsichord	Cembalo	Cembalo	Clavecin
Organ (Org.)	Organo	Orgel	Orgue

Appendix B

SOME TECHNICAL TERMS FREQUENTLY USED IN ORCHESTRAL SCORES

ENGLISH	ITALIAN	GERMAN	FRENCH
Muted; With mute(s)	Con sordino	mit Dämpfer; Gedämpft (for horns)	Sourdine(s)
Take off mutes	Via sordini	Dämpfer(n) Weg	Enlevez les sourdines
Without mute	Senza sordino	Ohne Dämpfer	sans sourdine
Divided	Divisi (div.)	Geteilt (get.)	Divisé(e)s (div.)
Divided in 3 parts (or whatever number is specified)	div. a 3	Dreifach	div. à 3
In unison (unis.)	Unisono (unis.)	Zusammen	Unis
Solo	Solo	Allein	Seul
All	Tutti	Alle	Tous
(First player only) 1.	1°	1ste; einfach	1er
1., 2. (first and second players on separate parts)	1°, 2°	1ste, 2te	1er, 2^{e}
a2 (2 players on same part)	a2	zu 2	à 2
Near the bridge	Sul ponticello	am Steg	sur le chevalet
Bow over the fingerboard	Sul tastiera; Sul tasto	am Griffbrett	sur la touche
With the wood of the bow	Col legno	mit Holz; col Legno	avec le bois
At the point of the bow	Punta d'arco	Spitze	Pointe; de la pointe
At the frog of the bow	al Tallone	am Frosch	du talon
Half (half of a string section is to play)	la metà	die Hälfte	la moitié
Stopped (horns)	Chiuso; chiusi	Gestopft	Bouché; bouchés
Open	Aperto; aperti	Offen	Ouvert
With soft stick; with soft mallet	Bacchetta di spugna	mit Schwammschlegel	Baguette d'éponge; baguette molle
With hard stick(s)	Bacchette di legno	mit Holzschlegeln	Baguette(s) en bois

(Directive to change tuning,
  or instrument):

Change C to E	Sol Muta in Mi	C nach E umstimmen	Changez Do en Mi
Change to piccolo (or whatever instr.)	Muta in Piccolo	Piccolo nehmen	Changez en piccolo
Stand, or Desk	Leggio	Pult	Pupitre
Ordinary; In ordinary way	Modo ordinario	Gewöhnlich	Mode ordinaire; position nat.

Ordinary; In ordinary way
  (play in ordinary manner, after
  having played sul ponticello,
  for example)

Appendix C

THE DEVELOPMENT OF WESTERN MUSIC: AN ANTHOLOGY VOLUME I, SECOND EDITION TO THIRD EDITION CONVERSION

The following conversion table will assist instructors who wish to continue using this anthology with texts other than the third edition of *The Development of Western Music: A History*. A dash signifies that the selection does not appear in that particular edition of the anthology.

VOL. I, 2D ED. DWMA No.	TITLE	VOL. I, 3D ED. DWMA No.	VOL. I, 2D ED. DWMA No.	TITLE	VOL. I, 3D ED. DWMA No.
1	Anon., *Hymn to Nikkal*	1	24	Anon., *Sumer is icumen in*	25
2	Anon., *First Delphic Hymn to Apollo*	2	25	Hildegard von Bingen, *Ordo virtutum* (excerpt)	26
3	*Epitaph of Seikilos*	3	26	Guiraut de Bornelh, *Reis glorios*	27
4	Anon., *Salve, Regina*	4	27	Raimbaut de Vaqueiras, *Kalenda maya*	28
5	Anon., *Missa in Dominica resurrectionis*	5	28	Guillaume d'Amiens, *Prendés i garde*	29
6	Anon., *Absolve, Domine*	6	29	Adam de la Halle, *Dieus soit*	30
7	Thomas of Celano, *Dies irae*	7	30	Anon., *A l'entrada del tens clar*	31
—	Anon., *Ecce Pater—Resurrexi*	8	31	Anon., *Or la truix*	32
8	Anon., *Quem quaeritis in sepulchro?*	9	32	Adam de la Halle, *Le Jeu de Robin et de Marion*, "Robins m'aime"	33
9	Guido d'Arezzo, *Ut queant laxis*	10			
10	Anon., *Early Organum*	11	33	Beatritz, *A chantar mes al cor*	34
—	Anon., *Alleluia, Justus ut palma*	12	34	Anon., *Cantigas de Santa Maria*	35
11	Anon., *Free Organum*	—	35	Anon., *Gloria 'n' cielo*	36
12	Anon., St. Martial style Organum, *Benedicamus*	13	36	Walter von der Vogelweide, *Palästinalied*	37
13	*Alleluia, Pascha nostrum*	14	—	Anon., Estampie from Robertsbridge Codex	38
14	Ato, *Nostra phalans*	15	37	de Vitry, *Garrit gallus—In nova fert—N[euma]*	39
15	Albertus, *Congaudeant catholici*	16	38	de Vitry, *Detractor est—Qui secuntur—Verbum iniquum*	40
16	Anon., *Regnat*	17	39	Machaut, *Messe de Nostre Dame, Agnus Dei*	41
17	Pérotin, *Alleluia, Nativitas*	18	40	Machaut, *Ma fin est mon commencement*	42
18	Pérotin, *Mors*	19	43	Jacopo da Bologna, *Non al suo amante*	43
19	Anon., *Veri floris*	20	44	Jacopo da Bologna, *Fenice fu' e vissi*	44
20	Anon., *Hac in anni ianua*	21	45	Gherardello da Firenze, *Tosto che l'alba*	45
21	Anon., *En non Diu—Quant voi—Eius in Oriente*	22	46	Landini, *Si dolce non sonò*	46
22	Anon., *Pucelete—Je languis—Domino*	23	47	Landini, *Non avrà ma' pietà*	47
23	Petrus de Cruce, *Aucuns vont souvent—Amor qui cor—Kyrie*	24	42	Anon., *Salve, sancta parens*	48

VOL. I, 2D ED. DWMA No.	TITLE	VOL. I, 3D ED. DWMA No.	VOL. I, 2D ED. DWMA No.	TITLE	VOL. I, 3D ED. DWMA No.
41	Dunstable, *Quam pulchra es*	49	86	Diruta, *El Transilvano: Toccata No. 13*	88
48	Du Fay, *Vergene bella*	50	87	G. Gabrieli, *In ecclesiis*	89
49	Du Fay, *Se la face ay pale*	51	88	Caccini, *Amarilli mia bella*	90
50	Du Fay, *Nuper rosarum flores—Terribilis est locus iste*	52	89	Corsi, *Dafne: "Bella ninfa fuggitiva"*	91
51	Du Fay, *Missa L' Homme armé, Agnus Dei*	53	90	Monteverdi, *Cruda Amarilli*	92
52	Binche (Binchois), *De plus en plus*	54	91	Monteverdi, *L' Orfeo: "Possente spirto"*	93
53	Ockeghem, *Missa Prolationum, Kyrie*	55	92	A. Scarlatti, *La Griselda: Act II, Scene 4*	94
54	Obrecht, *Parce, Domine*	56	93	Lully, *Alceste: Ouverture*	95
55	Josquin, *Ave Maria*	57		Purcell, *Dido and Aeneas:*	
56	Josquin, *Absalon, fili mi*	58	94	"Thy hand, Belinda"—"When I am laid in earth"	96
57	Isaac, *Zwischen Perg und tieffem Tal*	59	—	"With drooping wings"	96
58	Gombert, *Super flumina Babylonis*	60	95	Carissimi, *Jephte* (Conclusion)	97
59	Willaert, *Victimae paschali laudes*	61	96	Schütz, *Symphoniae sacrae, "O quam tu pulchra es"*	98
60	Morales, *Emendemus in melius*	62	97	Schütz, *Die sieben Worte . . . Jesu Christi am Kreuz, Introit*	99
61	Cara, *Oimè el cuor*	63	98	Sweelinck, *Fantasia chromatica*	100
62	Festa, *Quando ritrovo la mia pastorella*	64	99	Anon., *Canzona per l'epistola*	101
63	Rore, *Da la belle contrade d'oriente*	65	100	Froberger, *Suite XXII, E minor*	102
64	Marenzio, *Solo e pensoso*	66	101	Frescobaldi, *Toccata nona*	103
65	Gesualdo, *Moro, lasso, al mio duolo*	67	102	*Vater unser im Himmelreich*	104
66	Morley, *Sing we and chant it*	68	102a	S. Scheidt	104a
67	Wert, *Non è sì denso velo*	69	102b	Buxtehude	104b
68	Janequin, *À ce joly moys de may*	70	—	Pachelbel	104c
69	Le Jeune, *Revecy venir du printemps* (excerpt)	71	102c	J. S. Bach	104d
70	Morley, *April is in my mistress' face*	72	103	Frescobaldi, *Ricercar dopo il Credo*	105
71	Dowland, *In darkness let me dwell*	73	104	Jacquet de la Guerre, *Suite in D minor*	106
72a	Hassler, *Mein G'müth ist mir verwirret*	74a	105	Couperin, *Vingt-cinquième Ordre*	107
72b	J. S. Bach, *O Haupt voll Blut und Wunden*	74b	106	Corelli, *Sonata da camera, Op. 2, No. 4*	108
73	Encina, *Todos los bienes del mundo*	75	107	Corelli, *Sonata da chiesa, Op. 5, No. 1*	109
74	Byrd, *Ego sum panis vivus*	76	108	Vivaldi, *Concerto in A major, Op. 9, No. 2, mvts. 1, 2*	110
75	Palestrina, *Lauda Sion*, Motet	77	—	Telemann, *Musique de Table II, Quartet in D minor*	111
76	Palestrina, *Missa Lauda Sion*	78	109	Rameau, *Castor et Pollux: "Séjour de l'éternelle paix"*	112
77	Victoria, *O vos omnes*	79	110	Rameau, *L' Enharmonique*	113
78	Lassus, *Tristis est anima mea*	80	—	J. S. Bach, *Cantata No. 80, "Ein' feste Burg . . . ," mvt. 1*	114
79	G. Gabrieli, *Sonata pian' e forte*	81	111	J. S. Bach, *Jesu, meine Freude* (motet)	
80	Schlick, *Gaude Dei genetrix* (excerpt)	82	112	J. S. Bach, *St. Matthew Passion* (excerpts)	115
81	Cavazzoni, *Recercar Quarto*	83	112a	Nos. 69–70. Recitative: "Ach, Golgotha" Aria: "Sehet, Jesus hat die Hand"	115a
82	Merula, *La Strada*	84	112b	No. 73. Recitative: "Und siehe da, der Vorhang" Chorus: "Wahrlich, dieser ist Gottes Sohn gewesen"	115b
83a	Anon., *Gloria tibi trinitas*	85a	113	J. S. Bach, *Das wohltemperirte Klavier, Prelude and Fugue in C minor, BWV 847*	116
—	Tye, *In nomine* (Crye)	85b			
83b	Bull, *In nomine*	—			
84	Cabezón, *Diferencias sobre el canto llano del Caballero*	86			
85	Milán, *El Maestro: Fantasia No. 17*	87	114	J. S. Bach, *Durch Adams Fall ist ganz verderbt, BWV 637*	117

Vol. I, 2d ed. DWMA No.	Title	Vol. I, 3d ed. DWMA No.
——	Handel, *Giulio Cesare:* Act III, Scene 7	118
115	Handel, *Messiah* (excerpts)	119
115a	Accompanied recitative, *"Comfort ye"*	119a
115b	Aria, *"Every valley"*	119a
——	Chorus, *"And the Glory of the Lord"*	119b
115c	Chorus, *"All we like sheep"*	——

In the third edition, Vol. II begins with selection No. 120. In the second edition, Vol. I continues through selection No. 134b; Vol. II commences with No. 135.

Vol. I, 2d ed. DWMA No.	Title	Vol. II, 3d ed. DWMA No.
116	D. Scarlatti, *Sonata in D major, K. 119 (L. 415)*	120
117	C. P. E. Bach, *Symphony No. 3, F major, H. 665 (W. 183),* mvt. 1	121
118	G. B. Sammartini, *Symphony No. 32, F major*	122
119	J. V. A. Stamitz, *Sinfonia a 8, No. 1, D major,* mvt. 1	123
120	Pergolesi, *La serva padrona:* *"La conosco"*	124
121	Rousseau, *Le devin du village,* Act I, Scene 1	125

Vol. I, 2d ed. DWMA No.	Title	Vol. II, 3d ed. DWMA No.
122	J. C. Bach, Concerto, Op. 7, No. 5, E♭ major, mvt. 1	126
123	Mozart, Concerto No. 27, B♭ major, K. 595, mvt. 1	127
124	Gluck, *Orfeo ed Euridice:* excerpt from Act II, Scene 1	128
125	Gluck, *Orfeo ed Euridice:* *"Che farò senza Euridice?"*	129
126	Haydn, *Sonata No. 26,* mvt. 2	——
127	Haydn, String Quartet, Op. 33, No. 2, mvt. 1	130
128	Haydn, Symphony No. 104 (London), D major, mvt. 1	131
——	Mozart, *Le nozze di Figaro:* *"Susanna, or via sortite"*	132
129	Mozart, *Il Don Giovanni:* *"Madamina"*	133
130	Mozart, *Sonata in C minor, K. 457*	134
131	Billings, *"When Jesus Wept"*	135
132	Hopkinson, *"My gen'rous heart disdains"*	136
133	Antes, *Trio in E♭ major, Op. 3, No. 1,* mvt. 1	137
134	Antes, Aria and Anthem:	138
134a	*"Go, Congregation, Go"*	138a
134b	*"Surely He has borne Our Griefs"*	138b

Index